M000201874

REAL French for Travelers

K. B. Oliver

Author of *Magical Paris: Over 100 Things to do Across Paris*

and

A French Garden: The Loire Valley

Monceau Publishing

Table of Contents

Index of Vocabulary

Chapter 1

Real French for Travelers

Phrase books are better than nothing at all, but wouldn't you rather speak REAL French? With just a bit of regular time and effort, you can learn the basics of the French language, and that opens up a new world to you as you travel.

Question: How much French does one need to learn, just to take a trip to France?

Answer: It depends on what you want out of your trip. Don't get me wrong . . . you'll still enjoy your trip to France, simply because it's one of the most varied, fascinating, and delightful destinations on earth. You could go there every year and never run out of memorable places to see or experiences to savor in your memory. You don't need language for this . . .

. . . but what if you want more?

- What if you'd like to be able to ask for what you need in the language of your country hosts?
- What if you get lost and need to find your way but can't find someone who speaks English?
- What if you'd like to order in a restaurant without needing the smile and point method?
- What if you would like to have a simple conversation with a French person?

Are you someone who enjoys dipping *below* the surface of the culture, deeper than the average traveler who doesn't make such efforts?

You don't have to be fluent to do all these things. However, you'd be surprised to find out how much even a basic level of French language proficiency will enhance your travels and lead

9

you to want to make multiple trips to France, Quebec, or other French-speaking nations.

Making an effort in the French language will also go a long way to more positive interactions with the local people.

Here are more reasons to learn even just a basic level of French:

- You will feel more empowered instead of helpless if faced with a language situation you don't understand or in case of any difficulties you may run into.

- It is personally satisfying to get sentences from another language out of your mouth and be understood.

- Whatever French you learn for your trip is a foundation you'll build upon. Learning French can become a lifelong hobby instead of only a trip-oriented tool.

- You'll have greater understanding of the local culture and the ways of the French; you'll be able to read articles, programs and descriptions, or museum summaries (or at least make an informed guess about what they say) as opposed to being completely clueless (. . . and who likes being clueless?).

- Lastly (this may have little relevance now but much relevance in a few years), many studies have proven that learning a language, at whatever age, slows down the development of Alzheimer's. My oldest French student was 91. It's never too late.

Hopefully, these are more than enough reasons to learn the beautiful French language, REAL French. French is not a difficult language to learn. The grammar is logical and, once learned, largely predictable. The pronunciation is the hardest element (I will cover this), but once you know the rules of pronunciation, it also becomes much easier.

A *Real French* Book

REAL French for Travelers is unique in its approach. Along with full explanations of each grammar principle, travel-oriented dialogues will illustrate grammar in the types of situations you'll likely encounter. You'll see grammar in context.

Although this program was developed for an adult community college class, motivated travelers at *any* age can benefit greatly from it. Short chapters explain basic principles one at a time. Exercises will help mastery. Travel-oriented dialogues provide realistic conversations, giving you typical language structures. These will also include the grammar and vocabulary you will have just learned. You can use this book on your own or in a classroom setting.

REAL French for Travelers will cover the same grammar as an introductory French course, from articles all the way to the basic past tense. Completing this book will give you the tools you need to do more than just "survive" in France, which is better than simply memorizing phrases you don't understand. You'll learn *real* French.

Regions of France

Many travelers are familiar with Paris, though not necessarily other regions of France. When I say "familiar", that might be no more than a 1-day stopover, a romantic weekend, or a speedy one-week blitz. If that's all the time you've had, it's surely better than nothing! But it probably has given you a thirst for seeing more.

It's hard to describe how much there is to see all across France, with amazing variety from one end to the other. Each region has characteristic regional cuisine and beverages. Most have wine specialties, except Normandy which produces Calvados, its famous apple brandy and Brittany, with a beer-like beverage called cidre. Then there is cognac to the southwest and champagne to the east. That will appeal to the foodies among us. But there's much more in each region.

11

Normandy: Best known for D-Day landings and Second World War history, this area brims with cute bed and breakfast inns in gentle pastoral settings, and small but lively beach towns, like Etretat and Honfleur.

Alsace: Famous for passing back and forth between France and Germany over the centuries, this area has its own unique cuisine, architecture, and dialect. Cities like Strasbourg and Colmar, with canals and half-timbered buildings, will charm you as much as the flamenkuche and choucroute. (Hint: These are edible and you should really check them out!)

Provence offers more than lavender fields and upscale seaside resorts. There you'll see walled cities on cliff sides, small towns with tile roofs that make you feel like you're in a Marcel Pagnol novel, a sunny climate, and Mediterranean vibe.

The southwest has specialties like Bordeaux wine, cassoulet sausage stew, and Basque dishes. There are more seaside resort towns, like elegant Biarritz, long surfing and swimming beaches, and plenty of hiking, biking, and nature-oriented enjoyment.

The Loire Valley is often recognized for châteaux, which are scattered along the longest river in France. It is also an important wine region. Themed visits are popular here, including wine tours, castle visits...endless feasts of history and architecture.

Virtually anywhere you go, you will be rewarded with breathtaking scenery; quaint, memorable towns; and wonderful meals. Of course, this is not an exhaustive list. Don't forget the wine regions of the east, including Champagne, Bourgogne, and Alsace, or the Alps region, with its fondue and ski resorts.

In summary, there's simply too much to describe. If you want to experience the variety and bounty of France, you'll have a lot of trips to make. Having some French under your belt will definitely be a plus.

People, Culture, and Myths

The French people are one of the great natural resources of France. Of course, any country will have a few hot-tempered waiters or cashiers. But on a personal level, the French value their culture and their language, and if you make an effort to value them too, you'll meet a warm response.

Here are a few things to know about French people and culture:

- Like many Europeans, they may be reserved at first, but once you develop a relationship, they can be very warm.

- The French are logical and intellectual. They have a high regard for education, philosophy and individuality. Resistance and rebellion also figure in that list, as history has shown. They can be up for a good heated discussion over dinner, then walk away smiling, still friends.

- France is a very aesthetic culture. People generally dress with care and style, even when casual. They give a high importance to the arts, and this flows through many aspects of the culture. You may even see sculptures adorning the sidelines of highways.

- The French place a high value on family, friendship, vacations, free time, leisure, and security.

- And this is important to mention: The French do not dislike Americans. I'm not sure who started this rumor but it's simply not true. They don't always appreciate American politics, but that is another story.

Chapter 2

Pronunciation and Accents in French

French has very different rules for pronunciation than English. In addition, accents affect both written and, to a lesser degree, spoken French. Once you learn these new rules, you'll be able to predict the pronunciation of French words.

Vowels are important to understand in French pronunciation. The 5 vowels are the same letters as in English, but the sound is different.

a This is most often pronounced *ah*, whether it appears in the beginning or middle of a word. This will be influenced by whatever letters come directly after.

e When you see an *e* with no accent it is often pronounced **eu**. Think of the word "put". Try the word regarder (to look at) reu-gar-day.

i The i is pronounced ee.

o This is similar to the English o except it's sharper.

u The u sound (when not surrounded by other vowels) is a tight oo (ewe). Your lips are tighter together when you say it.

French vowels aren't long and short like in English does. There are a number of vowel combinations. These are important in determining the sound of a word. Here are some common ones:

au: pronounced oh. This can occur anywhere in the word.

ou: prounounced oo, with a wider sound. Vous, for example.

14

eu: This combination sounds like the e by itself, eu.

oi: The combination oi sounds like wah. Oiseau, poisson.

ui: Think of the word "oui", or yes. The ui vowel combination sounds like oo-ee but faster. Try them slowly, then faster.

ill: This combination is usually pronounced ee-yuh. Think of the words fille and famille. The few exceptions include ville (town), village (village), and mille (thousand.)

Accents

é (accent aigue) This is pronounced ay, as in **day**. (Note: There are other letter combinations that are pronounced the same way: er (for -ER verb infinitives), words ending in −et, and words conjugated −ez. An example is in the word occupé (busy), pronounced ohk-you-pay.

è is called accent grave, a softer sound "eh", like mère, "mare". Think of the word egg. That is the sound made by this accent.

c can have two sounds, the soft (S sound) or hard (K sound). The soft S sound occurs when the c is followed by e or i (examples: ceci, cinema.) The hard K sound occurs when the c is followed by a, o, or u (examples: casser, capacité, concert.)

Ç or ç This is called a cédille and gives an "s" sound to a C that would normally take the hard sound, those followed by a, o, or u. Ça (that) is pronounced **sah.**

ch is pronounced like sh. Chercher, to look for, is pronounced sher-shay.

Some sounds in French may seem hard to pronounce. If you look at the vowels in the word and review your pronunciation rules for vowels, it will help a lot.

A vowel followed by an **N** or **M** will always be nasal. (jambon, maison, pain, vin, etc.) See Appendix B for some audio resources for practice.

15

Chapter 3

Greetings and Polite Expressions

Many language learning methods begin with greetings. Greetings and polite expressions are worth learning right off the bat before you actually understand the grammar involved in those phrases. Why? Because you'll be using them right away and often, and it's important to be a polite traveler.

Let's get started!

HELLO

Bonjour means Hello (Good day or good morning) and can be said all day up until about 6 pm.

You can say this to strangers in stores as you enter (this seems strange to us, but is frequently done in France), but usually *not* to strangers outside on the streets.

Salut means hello or goodbye and is informal.

Around 6 pm you change to:

Bonsoir, or Good Evening.

Bonne nuit means Good Night and is only used when retiring to bed.

WHAT'S YOUR NAME?

Comment vous appelez-vous?

This phrases literally means "How do you call yourself?" or What's your name? In French there is a polite form (vous) and an informal form (tu) of "you". Normally you will use the polite form for every interaction with a person you don't know at all or very well.

16

Appeler is the verb "to call".

Je m'appelle _____. My name is ____ (or I call myself ___)

Et vous? (and you?) et is the word "and" and is pronounced like the letter A.

Comment vous appelez-vous? What's your name? (formal)

In French pronunciation, liaisons between words are frequent, especially when the second word begins with a vowel. When there is a verb that begins with a vowel, you slide the preceding consonant sound across. The s on vous is usually silent, but when followed by the verb "appelez", it sounds like a z so you say: commohn (nasal) voo-zap-e-lay voo.

In the informal, for "you", you'll say tu, with your lips more closed than for "too".

Comment t'appelles-tu? You'll only use this in the case of people much younger. If you aren't sure, always use vous.

HOW ARE YOU?

Comment allez-vous? How are you? (Literally: how are you going?) Formal

Comment vas-tu? Informal

Ça va? Very informal. Use with friends

Ways to respond:

Je vais bien, merci. I'm doing well, thanks.

Pas mal. Not bad.

Très bien, merci. Very well, thank you.

Comme ci, comme ça. So so.

Ça va. Good. (informal)

17

Don't forget to ask : **Et vous** ?   (informal: **et toi?**)

Other Polite Expressions

Merci: Thank you

S'il vous plait: Please (**s'il te plait** : informal please)

De rien: You're welcome   **Je vous en prie** (very formal)

Enchanté(e): Happy to meet you

Bonne journée: Have a good day.

Vous de même: To you the same.

Au revoir: Good bye

À bientôt: See you soon

À toute à l'heure, à plus tard: See you later (the same day)

Pardon, excusez-moi: Excuse me

Je suis désolé(e)de vous déranger: I'm sorry to disturb you

INTRODUCTIONS

Je vous présente ... (Then give the name of the person you are introducing) In the informal you can say **Je te présente** or   **c'est**

Sometimes other expressions are used for introductions, such as:

   Voici: here is

   Voilà: there is

These words are used in many other situations when someone wants to indicate something or someone nearby. Voilà also means "there it is", or "that's right."

18

Il y a is another expression which means "there is" or "there are", and carries the idea of existence. Il y a plusieurs portes ici. (There are several doors here, or several doors exist here.) Il y a is an expression made up of 3 separate words. Il, which you know as *it*, y is a pronoun, and a is a form of avoir, or to have (to be covered in Chapter 13). It's easier not to break it apart, so just learn it as an idiomatic unit.

Dialogue 1 *Greetings*

Formal

A: Bonjour, monsieur.

B : Bonjour, mademoiselle/madame/monsieur. Comment vous appelez-vous ?

A : Je m'appelle _____. Et vous ?

B : Je m'appelle _____.

A : Enchanté(e). Comment allez-vous ?

B : Très bien, merci. Vous êtes de Paris ?

A : Oui. Et vous ?

B : Non, je suis de Lyon.

A : Au revoir, monsieur/madame/mademoiselle

B : Bonne journée !

Informal

A : Salut. Comment vas-tu ?

B : Pas mal. Et toi ?

A : Je vais bien, merci.

B : Comment t'appelles-tu ?

A : Je m'appelle _____.

B : Ça va ?

A : Oui, ça va.

B : Salut.

TO DO: Try to write a dialogue similar to the one you just read. Use some of the same phrases and structures.

Chapter Four

Genders, Articles and Nouns

The French language has 2 genders, masculine and feminine. There isn't necessarily a logical reason for why something is masculine or feminine. There are some ways to predict the gender of certain words, while for other words, you simply have to memorize the gender. It is very important to learn the genders of nouns, since they influence many other parts of speech. The best thing is to learn the gender at the same time as you learn the definition of the word.

The word "the" in English is called a definite article. It is definite because the word "the" refers to a particular thing, as opposed to "a", which is general. Here are definite and indefinite articles in French:

Definite Articles

masculine: le   Example: le livre (the book)

feminine: la   Example : la pomme (the apple)

plural: les   Example: les amis (the friends) The same for both genders

There is a special form for singular words beginning with vowels: l'

Examples

l'appartement (the apartment) In this case you cannot tell by the article what the noun's gender is, so you'll have to learn this.

L'ami(e): the friend (masculine, feminine)

21

Indefinite Articles

Masculine: un   Example : un garçon (a boy)

Feminine: une   Example : une maison (a house)

Plural : des   Example : des bananes (some bananas)

4A. Here are some basic nouns with their genders shown by their articles. Supply the article, whether definite or indefinite.

Example : Une maison: a house

la fille _____ girl

le repas _____ meal

un bureau _____ office

le chien _____ dog

un vélo _____ bike

Determining Gender

As you learn more vocabulary, the words will get more complex. It would be nice to be able to guess the gender of certain nouns the first time you see them or want to use them. Many nouns do give a clue in their endings. Some endings will almost always be masculine, and others will almost always be feminine. This is a general rule, and there are exceptions.

Here are a few general guidelines:

MASCULINE NOUNS:

- Nouns that end in –isme, -oir, -teur, -ail, -al, -ier, -et, -ège

Examples

The –ism words, such as le tourisme, le terrorisme, le socialisme

-oir : un devoir (a duty), le pouvoir (power), un détail (a detail), un billet (a ticket), un hôpital (a hospital), un moteur (a motor), un ordinateur (a computer.)

-ier, -et, -ège : un clavier (a keyboard), un sommet (a summit), un privilège (a privilege)

- Nouns ending in –age, -ment, -o/-ot, -on, -eau, -ent)

Examples

--age: un voyage (a trip)

--ment: un département, un logement (department, housing)

--on: un melon, un jambon (melon, ham)

--ent: un talent, un parent (talent, parent)

--eau: un plateau (a tray), un bureau (office), un drapeau (a flag)

--age: le jardinage (gardening), un voisinage (a neighborhood)

-o, ot: le stylo: (the pen), un pivot (a pivot) un haricot (a bean)

- Most nouns that come from other languages are masculine. (eg le jogging, le shopping, le marketing, le yoga, le tennis.)

  FEMININE NOUNS:

- Nouns that end in –tié, -rie, -ance, -ence, -esse, -ette, -ise, -euse

23

--tié: une amitié (a friendship), une moitié (half)

--ance, --ence: une correspondance (a train connection, correspondence), une différence, une influence (exception: le silence)

-ette: une courgette (zuchini), une chaussette (sock)

--euse: une perceuse (a drill)

--ise: une crise (crisis), une bise (a kiss)

--esse: la jeunesse (youth), la finesse (finesse).

- Nouns ending in –ade, -ée, -ie, -ion, ité, -té, -ice

--ade: une promenade, une salade, une baignade (swimming excursion)

--ée: une journée (a day), une idée (an idea)

--ion: une décision (decision), une transition (transition)

--ité, té: une identité (identity), une activité (activity), la liberté (liberty), la quantité (quantity)

--ie: une librairie (a bookstore)

--ice: la directrice (the female director), calculatrice (calculator)

Pronunciation Tip

For all nouns beginning with a vowel, two things happen in pronunciation. First, the definite article le or la will become l', as in l'animal. Second, for plurals when you use les or des, the s sound slides across and sounds like a z. Les (z sound) animaux (layz-anee-moh).

4B. Supply the correct definite article (le or la) to the following nouns. Observe their endings to help you determine the gender of nouns. You can learn some new nouns at the same time!

1. _____ village (village)
2. _____ alliance (wedding ring, agreement)
3. _____ sonnette (doorbell)
4. _____ garage (garage)
5. _____ château (castle)
6. _____ jeunesse (youth)
7. _____ idéalisme (idealism)
8. _____ journal (newspaper)
9. _____ matinée (morning)
10. _____ mise à jour (update)
11. _____ quantité (quantity)
12. _____ billet (ticket)
13. _____ salon (living room)
14. _____ moment (moment)
15. _____ valise (suitcase)
16. _____ diversité (diversity)
17. _____ chapeau (hat)
18. _____ tennis (tennis)

Genders in using adjectives

Whenever you want to modify a noun with an adjective, you'll need to take into consideration the gender of the noun. Adjectives will be covered later on in Chapter 14, but for now it is important to know the basic formation of a feminine adjective, since that is the form likely to change.

- Most adjectives that describe a feminine noun simply add an "e" at the end of the word. This means that words that previously had a silent final consonant will now pronounce that final consonant.

- Sometimes the addition of an "e" doesn't change the pronunciation, only the spelling. This is true with words

25

like fatigué (tired) and occupé (busy). These words already have an accented e. The feminine form adds another e.

- Not all adjectives change when describing a feminine noun. For example, you could say "Ma mère est triste." (My mother is sad.) Triste does not change in the feminine form. It already has a non-accented e. Some others that don't change are malade (sick), sympa or sympatique (nice), and timide (shy).

- If you have an adjective that ends in –eux, the feminine form will have the ending –euse. Examples : heureux (happy) becomes heureuse. Délicieux becomes délicieuse, and sérieux becomes sérieuse.

Useful Nouns *(with definite articles)*

la fille: girl, daughter

la maison: house

le vélo: bike

le stylo: pen

la porte: door

le chat: cat

le chien: dog

le livre: book

le vin: wine

la banque: bank

la fleur: flower

la forêt: forest

la main: hand

le monde: world

le temps: time

l'idée (f): idea

la voiture: car

l'homme: man

le travail: work

la fenêtre: window

la chaise: chair

la table: table

le cahier: notebook

la personne: person

les gens: people

l'ami (e): friend

le repas: meal

Chapter 5

Plurals

French nouns are relatively easy to make plural. Normally you only need to add an "s" to the word.

la fille: the girl   The plural becomes les filles, the girls.

le livre....les livres   The books.

l'homme...les hommes   The men.

The pronunciation of words in the plural doesn't usually sound different than in the singular (though there are exceptions, which you'll see later). That means you'll have to **clearly** pronounce the plural article "les" or "des" to indicate that you are speaking of a plural. Just for practice, say the words "le" and "les" (luh and lay) several times and notice the difference.

In pronouncing a plural word that begins with a vowel, there is a pronunciation difference. You pronounce the previous s in "les" like a z sound and this sound slides over to the vowel word. For example, les hommes (the men)   Layz-um.

If a word ends in s, x, or z, you do not need to add s for a plural form. For example, the word fils (son) stays the same in the plural, as does the word nez (nose).

Special Forms

Sometimes there are special forms for the plural. If a singular noun ends in –**eau**, like château (castle), drapeau (flag), or chapeau (hat), the plural form adds an x instead of an s. So in the plural you will have châteaux, drapeaux, and chapeaux.

Words that end in –**al**, like animal (animal), l'hôpital (hospital), and journal(newspaper) also take X in the plural form.

Les animaux, les hôpitaux, and les journaux. Don't forget the liaison when needed. Remember the –aux is pronounced "oh".

Other irregular endings for plurals include these:

--**ieu** as in lieu (place) becomes lieux. There is no change in pronunciation.

The masculine form is used for a group of people, or a general designation, like étudiant for student. A female student will be une étudiante. For some words you'll add an "e" for the feminine form, unless there is already an e. This is also the case for a person of a particular nationality. Often the feminine form will have an e or some alternate ending (such as une Américaine, une Tunisienne, une Italienne for females from those countries). Of course, for plurals you would add an s after the e.

Practice pronouncing these pairs of words:

- un homme vs. des hommes   (a man, some men)
- une amie vs. des amies (a friend, some friends, both female)
- la maison vs. les maisons   (the house, the houses)
- un train vs. des trains (a train, some trains)
- l'appartement vs. les appartements   (the apartment, the apartments)

5A. In the following words, make the plurals into singulars, and the singulars into plurals. Pay attention to both the word endings and articles. (Keep definite and indefinite articles the same).

1.	la fille *examples :*	les filles	(girl, daughter)
2.	des livres	un livre	(books)
3.	des histoires		(stories)
4.	un gâteau		(cake)
5.	le poisson		(fish)
6.	des bouteilles		(bottles)

29

7. le chapeau   (hat)

8. un parc   (park)

9. l'hôpital   (hospital)

10. un bureau   (office)

11. un choix   (choice)

12. les voisins   (neighbors)

13. un journal   (newspaper)

14. les fenêtres   (window)

15. le fils   (son)

Chapter 6

Etre: To Be

The first verb you will usually learn in any language program is the verb "to be", a basic building block of communication. In French, the word "to be" is "être". It is irregular and therefore has an unusual conjugation. However, you will use it so frequently that you'll learn it quickly.

être: to be

je suis (I am)	nous sommes (we are)
tu es (you are, informal)	vous êtes (you are, formal or plural you)
il, elle, on est (he, she, it, one is)	ils, elles sont (they are, masculine/mixed, feminine)

Pronouns : In the above section you will also see the pronouns: je (I), tu (you, informal), il (he, it), elle (she, it), on (one, the impersonal "they" or, in informal speech, "we.") Then in plural you have nous (we), vous (you, formal or plural) and ils (male or mixed, plural) and elles (feminine plural).

Now, let's make some sentences. But we'll have to add another element, adjectives. In the adjectives below, the second form is feminine. More on feminine and masculine in adjectives later on. For now, let's start with these:

timide: shy	sympathique, sympa: nice, friendly
malade: sick	intelligent(e): intelligent
occupé(e): busy	fatigué(e): tired
sportif/sportive: athletic	laid(e): ugly

31

content(e): content	méchant(e): mean
amical(e): friendly	têtu(e): stubborn
bon/bonne: good	facile: easy
beau/belle: attractive handsome, beautiful,	difficile: difficult

6A. Create a few sentences for practice. Don't forget to add an e if needed for feminine, and an s if needed for plural. You can use other nouns as subjects as well.

Examples Ils sont têtus. (They are stubborn.) Les garçons sont sympas. (The boys are nice.)

Nous....

Les chiens ....

Elles ....

Vous....

Les voisins (neighbors) ....

Les gens (people) ......

Le gâteau (cake) .....

La maison ....

Tu ....

6B Translate the phrases below into French.

The cake is delicious.   *Example* Le gâteau est délicieux.

We are tired.

The neighbors are rich.

32

The boy is timid.

The man is intelligent.

You (informal) are interesting.

The woman is sick.

You (plural) are stubborn.

Some expressions using être

être en avance: to be early   *Example* Elle est en avance.

être en retard: to be late

être en vacances: to be on vacation

être en colère: to be angry

être de bonne/mauvaise humeur: to be in a good/bad mood

être à l'heure: to be on time

être de retour: to be back or on the way back from somewhere

être d'accord: to be in agreement

être en train de + infinitive verb: to be in the process of doing something

Chapter 7

Numbers, Months, and Seasons

<u>Numbers:</u>   1-31

un/e	one	seize	sixteen
deux	two	dix-sept	seventeen
trois	three	dix-huit	eighteen
quatre	four	dix-neuf	nineteen
cinq	five	vingt	twenty
six	six	vingt et un/e	twenty-one
sept	seven	vingt-deux	twenty-two
huit	eight	vingt-trois	twenty-three
neuf	nine	vingt-quatre	twenty-four
dix	ten	vingt-cinq	twenty-five
onze	eleven	vingt-six	twenty-six
douze	twelve	vingt-sept	twenty-seven
treize	thirteen	vingt-huit	twenty-eight
quatorze	fourteen	vingt-neuf	twenty-nine
quinze	fifteen	trente	thirty
		trente et un/e	thirty-one

7A. Take a minute now to read through all 31 of the numbers. Do this two times, then try to do it without looking at the list.

7B Now take a minute to write out all of the numbers, paying special attention to hyphens.

Months of the Year : Les mois de l'année

Months are not capitalized in French

janvier	(January)
février	(February)
mars	(March)
avril	(April)
mai	(May)
juin	(June)
juillet	(July)
août	(August)
septembre	(September)
octobre	(October)
novembre	(November)
décembre	(December)

En juillet :   In July

En décembre : In December

35

However, for holidays the rule is different: à Noël (at Christmas), à Pâques: at Easter

Dates

A date is typically expressed like this:

- Le 10 août, 2015. Always give the day first, preceded by the masculine definite article.

- Written short form: 10/08/15 (Note the day is *first* and the month *second* when expressed numerically)

- Nous sommes le 10 août. C'est le 10 août. It is the tenth of August.

- Je suis né(e) le 10 août. I was born on August 10.

- If you say the first, use premier. C'est le premier août. It's the first of August.

Seasons

All 4 season names are masculine. However, since all but spring begin with a vowel, they use the definite article l' and en.

l'hiver (winter) en hiver (in winter)

le printemps (spring) au printemps (in spring)

l'été (summer) en été (in summer)

l' automne (in autumn) en automne (in autumn)

la saison : the season

For Days of the week, see page 44.

36

Chapter 8

The 3 Regular Verb Forms / -ER Verbs

In French as in English there are both regular and irregular verbs. You have already met one irregular French verb, être.

There are 3 main forms of **regular** verbs in French, and these are all identified by their endings. They end in -ER, in -IR, and in -RE.

The first category, -ER verbs, is the most common. These are easy to conjugate because they always follow the same form. Also, the first, second, third person singular and third person plural are all pronounced the same way.

We'll see an example with the word "marcher", which means "to walk". In French, je marche can mean I walk or I am walking.

je marche (I walk)   nous marchons (we walk)

tu marches (you walk) informal   vous marchez (you walk) pl,
                                                            formal

il, elle marche (he, she walks)   ils, elles marchent (they walk)
                                      masculine, feminine

If you take off the -ER, what's left is known as the "stem". On the stem, you place the endings: -e,- es,-e, -ons, -ez, and -ent.

Here's another one: danser (to dance)

          je dans**e**   nous dans**ons**

          tu dans**es**   vous dans**ez**

          il, elle, on dans**e**   ils, elles dans**ent**

37

Do not ever pronounce the "-ent" of the plural 3rd person. Most verbs will use the same plural endings of "-ons", "-ez", and "-ent". It's one nice, predictable thing about French!

Here are some additional -ER verbs

Note that some of these verbs have accompanying prepositions.

regarder: to watch

déjeuner: to eat lunch

travailler: to work

manger: to eat

arriver: to arrive

jouer (à la, au) : to play a sport

parler (à): to talk to

parler (de): to talk about

rester: to stay

préparer: to prepare

aimer: to like, to love

écouter: to listen to

acheter: to buy

chercher: to look for

visiter: to visit (a place)

habiter: to live

jouer (de la, du) : to play a musical instrument

inviter (à): to invite someone (to do something)

Some English verbs will require prepositions while French equivalents do not (such as look *at*, sit *down*). The opposite is also true. In French sometimes a preposition à or de will be needed between 2 verbs, and sometimes before a noun. It's easier to learn these at the same time you learn the verb.

8A Take a moment to choose 5 of the above verbs and practice writing out their conjugations on a blank piece of paper.

Chapter 9

Aller: To Go

Aller is one of the irregular verbs you will use most frequently. It has an unusual conjugation, but you'll use this verb often.

je **vais**	nous **allons**
tu **vas**	vous **allez**
il, elle, on **va**	ils, elles **vont**

Some of the forms of aller should look familiar to you. Remember the expressions "Comment allez-vous" and "Ça va"? These greetings which you learned in Chapter 3 use the verb aller.

If you want to say you are going somewhere, in English just as in French you often say "to" or "to the...". In French if you want to say "to" you use à and then use the definite article. You'll remember that definite articles are either masculine or feminine, so you'll use à la or au (which is a + le) depending on the gender of the place you are going.

Examples:

Je vais au musée. (I'm going to the museum. Musée is masculine, so use au.)

Mes voisins vont à la bibliothèque tous les jours. (My neighbors go to the library every day.) Library, bibliothèque, is feminine, so use à la.

Compare with the following phrase:

Nous allons à l'église chaque semaine. (We go to church every week.)

Eglise is feminine, therefore à la, but since église starts with a vowel, use à l'. The same will be true for a masculine noun starting with a vowel. Nous allons à l'appartement. (We're going to the apartment.)

Examples

Tu vas trop souvent au café. (You go to the café too often.)

Ils vont à Montréal cet été. (They are going to Montreal this summer) Use à with city names.

Mon cousin va au travail ce samedi. (My male cousin is going to work this Saturday.)

Some place names in French

le musée	museum
l'église (f)	church
l'école (f)	school
le marché	open market
la bibliothèque	library
la librairie	book store
le stade	stadium
le travail	work
le bureau	the office
le supermarché	supermarket
le magasin	store (general name)
le grand magasin	department store
la boutique	small specialty store
le parc	park
la piscine	swimming pool
l'appartement (m)	apartment
la boulangerie	bakery
la boucherie	butcher shop
le cinéma	movie theater
le restaurant	restaurant
le théâtre	theater (for stage plays)

9A. Complete the following sentences for practice, using the correct form of aller and the correct gender for your preposition. (à la or au)

Example Tu <u>vas au</u> cinéma.

1. Il _____ _____ piscine.

2. Nous _____ _____ restaurant

3. Je _____ _____ école.

4. Les enfants _____ _____ parc.

5. Vous _____ _____ stade.

6. On _____ _____ supermarché.

7. Je _____ _____ boutique de chaussures (shoes).

8. Ma mère _____ _____ boulangerie acheter une baguette.

9. La professeur _____ _____ bureau.

10. Nous _____ tous (all)_____ travail.

Going To... Places

- When you say you are going to a city, always use the preposition **à**.
  Je vais à Nice la semaine prochaine. (I'm going to Nice next week.)

- When going to a country, use **en** for feminine countries or states, as well as those beginning with a vowel, and **au** for masculine countries or states. There is no rhyme or reason to genders of place, though most that end in E are

42

feminine. An exception is le Mexique. Most countries ending in other letters are masculine. It's best to learn the names of countries and states that you use the most often.

Examples

Mes amis vont en France pour les vacances. (My friends are going to France for vacation.)

Il va au Canada chaque année. (He goes to Canada each year.)

- When you are coming from somewhere, use the irregular verb "venir" (to come) with the preposition "de". Il vient du Canada. (He comes from Canada. Use "du" because de + le = du, in the masculine). Venir is on page 100.

- The word revenir means to come back and is conjugated like venir.

- You can use the same expression to say you come from a particular country. Je viens des Etats-Unis. (I come from the United States. Use 'des' because States is plural.)

- To express "from" with a feminine country or state, use de or d' with no article. For cities, use de or d' as well.

Ils viennent de France. (They come from France.)
Nous venons de New York. (We come from New York.)

43

During the Week

Here is some new vocabulary to help you describe your daily or weekly activities.

la semaine: the week

chaque semaine: each week

parfois: sometimes

régulièrement: regularly

d'habitude: usually

souvent: often

le matin: morning

l'après-midi: afternoon

le soir: evening

la nuit: night

Days of the week: In French these are not capitalized

lundi: Monday

mardi: Tuesday

mercredi: Wednesday

jeudi: Thursday

vendredi: Friday

samedi: Saturday

dimanche: Sunday

When you express doing something regularly, use "le" before the day.

Example

Le samedi je vais au marché. On Saturdays, I go to the market.

44

9B. Write 5 phrases to describe your habits using the above vocabulary.

Example   Le lundi matin je vais à la piscine. (On Monday mornings, I go to the pool.)

Going to.... Intention

Sometimes we use the phrase "going to" with another verb to talk about something we're going to do soon. I'm going to see a movie, for example. You can do the same thing in French. This is often called futur proche, or near future.

Examples

Je vais acheter des légumes. (I'm going to buy some vegetables.)

Tu vas étudier ce soir? (Are you going to study this evening?)

Les enfants vont jouer dans le jardin. (The children are going to play in the yard.)

9C. Your turn: Create 6 sentences using *aller* plus another verb from the -ER verb list in Chapter 8.

Daily Habits   **Dialogue 2a**

(Feel free to substitute your own name)

Anne: Bonjour, Pierre. Comment allez-vous?

Pierre : Bonjour, Anne. Très bien, merci. Et vous ?

Anne :   Pas mal. J'achète des affaires (some things) pour les
          vacances. Nous allons à Montpellier.

Pierre : C'est bien! Je vais à la montagne. J'aime être à la
          campagne.

Anne :   Nous restons à l'hôtel à Montpellier. Nous y allons
          mercredi.

Two Friends discuss their activities   **Dialogue 2b**

Sophie :   Chaque semaine je vais à la piscine. Et toi ?

Bruno :   Je n'aime pas la piscine. Je vais au parc. Parfois
           je mange un sandwich là-bas.

Sophie :   C'est intéressant. Le lundi je vais au magasin et
           le jeudi je danse. Le samedi je reste dans le
           quartier.

Bruno :   Tu es très occupée!

Additional vocabulary

La campagne: the countryside   là-bas: there, over there

Le quartier: the neighborhood, the area

occupé(e): busy   nous y allons: we're going there

TO DO: Try to write a dialogue using one of the above dialogues
         as a model. Use some of the same structures and phrases.

47

Chapter 10

Conjunctions, Words of Frequency, and Small Words

When learning a new language, it's often the little words that throw us off. The little things we forget can change meaning. Knowing them can enable us to say just what we want to say. Here is a list of some little words you will want to know:

Alors: This is a word that means "so", for a cause/effect situation. For example: I was running late, so I caught a taxi. It's a filler word too, as is the English word "so". Just don't overuse it.

J'ai de nouveaux voisins, alors je fais un gâteau. (I have some new neighbors, so I'm making a cake for them.)

mais: but	avec: with
d'accord: agreed; okay	ici: here
sans: without	sur: on (top of), on the subject of
assez: enough; rather	moins de: fewer, less
ou: or	aussi: also
là: there	dans: in (inside of)
puis: then (in a series)	si: if, so, or yes to negative affirmation
parfois: sometimes	pourtant, cependant: however
maintenant: now	très: very trop, trop de : too, too much of
souvent: often	un peu: a little

beaucoup (de): a lot (of) d'habitude: usually

de: from, of c'est: it's...

des: some il y a: there is, there are

voici: here is, are voilà: there is, there are (visible)

avant: before après: after

rarement: rarely jamais: never

toujours: always aujourd'hui: today

ne (+ verb) pas: negative (covered in Chapter 13.)

en : in, to (for seasons, except printemps; for feminine countries, and in certain expressions; je vais en France (I'm going to France), modes of transportation: Je viens en voiture, or I'm coming by car. (Exceptions: à pied, by foot, à velo, by bike, à cheval, on horseback). There are other meanings as well.

10A. Read the following short story below in English, then in the French version, supply the missing "little words". Hint: these will come from the list just above.

In spring, I like to go to the beach. There are fewer people and today it isn't too hot. Usually I go with some friends. Today, however, I'm going there alone. There is a nice sunshine and a little bit of wind. Before arriving, I buy a sandwich to have a picnic. It's really pleasant to have a picnic on the sand.

When I have enough sun, I go home, but this time I'm going to see my friend. He's going to order a pizza with salad and we are going to watch a movie. We always have a good time together.

49

_____ printemps, j'aime aller _____ plage. Il y a _____ gens et aujourd'hui il ne fait pas _____ chaud. _____ j'y vais avec des amis. Aujourd'hui, _____, j'y vais seul. _____ un beau soleil et _____ de vent. _____ d'arriver, j'achète un sandwich pour faire un pique-nique. _____ _____ agréable de prendre un pique-nique _____ le sable.

Quand j'ai _____ soleil, je rentre chez moi, _____ cette fois-ci je vais voir mon ami. Il va commander une pizza _____ salade et nous allons regarder un film. Nous passons _____ un bon moment ensemble.

Chapter 11

Regular -IR verbs

The second category of regular verbs are verbs ending in -IR. These verbs have different conjugations from the -ER verbs, but generally all -IR verbs are conjugated alike. Here are some examples:

Finir: to finish

je finis	nous finissons
tu finis	vous finissez
il, elle, on finit	ils, elles finissent

Choisir : to choose

je choisis	nous choisissons
tu choisis	vous choisissez
il, elle, on choisit	ils, elles choisissent

Note: Use **de** before a second verb for both choisir and finir.

Ils choisissent de changer la moquette. (They choose to change the carpet.)

Alain finit d'écrire son roman. (Alain is finishing writing his novel.)

51

-IR verbs in sentences:

réfléchir à (reflect about)   use à before a noun or verb

Le directeur réfléchit aux options. (The director considers the options).

remplir (fill)

Le jeune homme remplit le seau pour arroser les fleurs. (The young man fills the bucket to water the flowers).

réussir à (succeed, manage to) use with a noun or verb

Il réussit à trouver la station. (He manages to find the station).

agir (to act)   réagir (to react)

Quand la route est dangereuse, il agit vite. (When the road is dangerous, he acts quickly).

11A   Practice with -IR verbs. Translate sentences into French.

1.   They are choosing a color for the house.

2.   We will finish the project before the evening.

3.   You fill out the paper.

4.   I am thinking about his idea. (son idée)

5.   The boys manage to finish the program. (le programme)

Chapter 12

Avoir: To Have

One of the most common and important irregular verbs in French is the verb "avoir", or "to have". The conjugation is not predictable, so you'll need to memorize it. However, you'll use it so often you will remember it quickly.

j'ai   (I have)   nous avons (we have)

tu as (you have)   vous avez (you have) plural or formal

il, elle, on a (he, she, one has)   ils, elles ont (they have) masculine and feminine

Examples:

Ils ont beaucoup de voitures. (They have a lot of cars.)

J'ai deux sœurs. (I have two sisters.)

Tu as une tache sur ton pull. (You have a stain on your sweater.)

Nous avons un rendez-vous à quinze heures. (We have an appointment at three o'clock.)

12A   Try the following sentences with the correct form of avoir:

1. Ils _____ deux chats.(two cats)

2. Nous _____ très peu de temps. (very little time)

53

3. J' _____ du travail dans un restaurant.

4. Vous _____ des enfants ?

5. Il _____ souvent des amis chez lui.

6. Tu _____ de beaux cheveux. (pretty hair.)

Some idioms that use the word AVOIR:

- Avoir chaud: to be hot (a person)

  J'ai chaud. (I am hot.) Note: Things can be called hot using être. La viande est chaude. The meat is hot. Same applies to cold; Add e if using a feminine noun.

- Avoir froid: to be cold   Les filles ont froid ce soir. (The girls are cold tonight.)

- Avoir faim: to be hungry   J'ai faim. Je veux manger quelque chose. (I'm hungry. I want to eat something.)

- Avoir besoin de: to need   J'ai besoin de stylo. (I need a pen.)

- Avoir soif : to be thirsty   Tout le monde a soif parce qu'il fait chaud. (Everyone is thirsty because it is hot.) Note : Il fait chaud or froid speaks of the weather. The verb is faire, to make or do.

- Avoir raison: to be right   Je sais qu'il a raison. (I know that he is right.)

- Avoir tort: to be wrong   Sur ce sujet, tu as tort.   (On this subject, you are wrong.)

- Avoir envie de: to want (have a craving or be in the mood for something)

54

- J'ai envie de manger de la glace. (I'm in the mood, feel like, to eat some ice cream.)

- <u>Avoir lieu</u>: to take place (impersonal) La cérémonie a lieu ce samedi. (The ceremony takes place this Saturday.)

- <u>Avoir l'air</u> : to look like   Tu as l'air triste. (You look sad.)

- <u>Avoir peur de</u>: to be afraid of   Mon fils a peur des chiens. (My son is afraid of dogs.)

- <u>Avoir l'intention de</u> + verb: to intend to do something, to plan on something. J'ai l'intention de nettoyer le garage. (I intend to clean the garage.)

12 B   Draw a line between the French expression on the left and the English translation on the right.

J'ai une mauvaise note.	You are always right.
La fête a lieu vendredi soir.	The boys want pizza.
Les garçons ont envie de pizza.	We're hot! Open the window!
Nous avons besoin de clés.	You look depressed. What's wrong?
Elle a souvent froid.	I have a bad grade.
On a chaud ! Ouvrez la fenêtre !	We need some keys.
Tu as l'air déprimé. Qu'est-ce qu'il y a ?	The party takes place Friday night.
Vous avez toujours raison.	She's often cold.

Avoir and Age

In French the word avoir is used when expressing age. Observe the following examples:

J'ai 32 ans. I am 32 years old. (literally: I have 32 years.)

Quel age avez-vous? (How old are you?)

Always use the word "ans", or years, after the number expressing your age or someone else's.

See Chapter 7 for numbers 1-31 and Chapter 20 for numbers up to 60. In Chapter 24 you'll find numbers up to 100, as well as rules for expressing dates.

56

Chapter 13

Negatives

Expressing a phrase in the negative is not difficult in French. The negative is in 2 parts and surrounds the verb like a sandwich. In its simplest form, it is ne + verb + pas. Look at the following examples:

Mon frère **ne** mange **pas** d'huîtres. (My brother doesn't eat oysters.)

Je **n'**aime **pas** les anchois. (I don't like anchovies.) The ne drops its e before a vowel.

La famille **ne** part **pas** en vacances. (The family isn't leaving on vacation.)

Practice with Negatives

13A Make the following positive sentences negative.

1. Les filles dansent très souvent. (often)

2. La lampe est jolie.

3. D'habitude (usually) ce magasin est ouvert.

4. Charles parle beaucoup.

5. Nous marchons dans le parc.

Other types of negative phrases:

There are several other types of negative expressions that follow the same form as ne...pas.

ne...plus (no longer) Elle ne travaille plus ici. (She doesn't work here anymore.)

ne...rien (nothing) Il ne voit rien dans le jardin. (He doesn't see anything in the yard.)

ne...jamais (never) Les voisins ne disent jamais 'bonjour'. (The neighbors never say hello.)

ne...personne (no one) Je n'invite personne. (I'm not inviting anyone.)

The previous expressions use the same word order as ne...pas.

• The words rien and personne can also be subjects, as in the following examples: Personne ne vient à la reunion. (No one is coming to the meeting.) Rien n'est cher ici. (Nothing is expensive here.)

• The expression "me either" is "moi non plus."

• If you use a verb in the negative with an *indefinite* article and a noun, the article changes to "de." De is a bit like saying "any". (Rule doesn't apply with être or with definite articles.)

Example: Il n'y a pas de café. There isn't any coffee.

Example : Je n'achète pas de pommes. I'm not buying apples.

• There are a few expressions that use "pas" without ne:
Pas moi   (not me)
Pas encore   (not yet)
Pas du tout   (not at all)
Pas de problème   (no problem) To say the same thing, as 'no problem', you can say: Ce n'est pas grave (It's not serious)

You can also use non (no) by itself in certain expressions :

Non, merci   (no, thank you)
J'espère que non. (I hope not.)

58

13B Translate the following sentences, using the best negative.

1. My neighbors never work in the yard.

2. I don't have the time to (de) watch the program (l'emission)

3. There is no more snow in front of the house.

4. I don't see anyone at the cash register. (la caisse)

5. We don't study over (pendant) the weekend

6. Ellen doesn't have any more orange juice.

7. There isn't anyone in this chair.

8. My son never finishes his homework.

9. She has nothing in her pockets. (dans ses poches.)

10. There isn't anything good (de bon) on television tonight.

11. My boss (mon chef) never tells the truth. (la vérité)

Chapter 14

Adjectives

Adjectives are words that describe something. In the phrase "A lovely sunset", the word lovely is an adjective. In French, the adjective normally comes after the noun.

For example, you might say, Elle a une maison moderne. (She has a modern house.)

Elle porte sa robe rouge. (She is wearing her red dress.)

Nous avons des amis intelligents. (We have intelligent friends.)

You can also express an adjective this way using the verb être, or to be: La fille est très jeune. (The girl is very young.)

Mon chat est vieux et gris. (My cat is old and gray.)

When using adjectives, you usually have to change the ending for feminine and for plurals.

- Often for <u>feminine</u> nouns, you simply add an **e** to the adjective. Vert/verte, grand/grande, for example.

- For <u>plurals</u>, you usually add an **s** to the adjective. Note the different spellings for "vert", green.

Le vélo vert	The green bike
La maison verte	The green house
Les vélos verts	The green bikes
Les maisons vertes	The green houses

*Examples*L

Les voisins ont deux chiens **noirs**. (The neighbors have two black dogs.)

60

Here there is an s added for a plural, but there's no change in pronunciation.

Mes sœurs ont des chambres **séparées**. (My sisters have separate bedrooms.)

In this example there is an e and an s added to séparé because chambre is feminine, and there are two of them.

You'll see different patterns for adjectives:

e added, no change in pronunciation. This happens when the final letter is already an accented **e**.

La femme occupée   The busy woman

Other examples: fatigué, désolé, séparé (tired, sorry, separate.)

e added for feminine, change in pronunciation. The final letter is a consonant. When you add an e for feminine, you will pronounce the consonant, though the e remains silent.

La voiture verte	The green car	vert, verte
Une idée intelligente	An intelligent idea	intelligent, intelligente
Un film intéressant	An interesting movie	intéressant, intéressante
Une dame française.	A French lady	français, française
Des voisines bavardes	Some talkative neighbors (female)	

No change for gender, change for plural

Le garçon triste.   The sad boy

Les films tristes   Sad movies

61

Other examples of adjectives that don't change for feminine because of a final **e**: sympathique (nice), malade (sick), timide (shy, timid).

Masculine plural: no change in pronunciation

Les hommes importants.   The important men.   S added for plural.

Note that sometimes in the plural, there will be no change in pronunciation of the adjective. Therefore, it is very important to pronounce clearly the "les" so that your listener will understand you are talking about a plural noun.

Exceptions

Although most adjectives that modify feminine nouns simply add e, a couple of categories have different endings.

-eux. When you have an adjective that ends in –**eux,** such as heureux (happy), paresseux (lazy), sérieux (serious), délicieux (delicious), for the feminine you will add a different ending, -euse. The final s here is pronounced like a z.

heureux becomes heureuse.

paresseux becomes paresseuse.

délicieux becomes délicieuse.

sérieux, dangereux, chanceux become sérieuse, dangereuse, chanceuse.

You'll find some other exceptions in nationality adjectives (which are not capitalized in French). Note masculine and feminine forms:

italien/ italienne

tunisien/tunisienne

américain/ américaine

français/ française

anglais/ anglaise

Some common adjectives have <u>irregular forms</u> in the feminine.

Masculine	Meaning	Feminine
• Blanc	(white)	blanche
• Faux	(false)	fausse
• Frais	(fresh, cool)	fraîche
• Long	(long)	longue
• Sec	(dry)	sèche
• Gros	(fat, big)	grosse

14A Supply the correct adjective for the following nouns: (See more adjectives on the next page).

1. (The intelligent boys) Les garçons

_____

2. (An interesting book) Un livre

_____

3. (The white sheet of paper) Une feuille

_____

4. (Some blue shoes) Des chaussures

_____

5. (A cool morning) Un matin

_____

63

6. (The Tunisian woman) Une femme

_____

7. (A lazy dog) Un chien

_____

8. (A French newspaper) Un journal

_____

9. (A dry road) Une rue

_____

10. (The sad man) Un homme

_____

Useful adjectives

agréable: pleasant	avare: stingy
cher (chère) expensive, dear	costaud(e) : sturdy, well-built (person)
drôle: funny	facile: easy
formidable: fabulous	pauvre: poor
sincère: sincere	sociable: friendly
timide: shy, timid	idéaliste: idealistic
difficile: difficult	optimiste: optimistic
stressé(e): stressed	calme: calm

réservé(e): reserved

nerveux/nerveuse: nervous

dynamique: dynamic

sportif/sportive: athletic

moche: ugly (slang)

maigre: skinny

fier/fière: proud

naïf/naïve: naïve

méchant(e): mean

bête: stupid

intelligent(e): intelligent

désolé(e) : sorry

têtu(e): stubborn

paresseux/paresseuse: lazy

discipliné(e): disciplined

généreux/ généreuse : generous

laid(e): ugly

mince: thin

raisonable: reasonable

gros/grosse: fat

sérieux/ sérieuse: serious

égoïste: selfish

dernier/dernière : last, final

excellent(e) : excellent

Colors

blanc/blanche : white

gris(e) : gray

jaune: yellow

orange: orange*

vert(e): green

bleu clair: light blue*

bleu foncé: dark blue (invariable)

brun(e): dark-haired, brown

bleu(e) : blue

rose : pink

marron: brown*

rouge: red

violet(te): purple

blond(e): blond

noir(e): black

65

*these words don't change with gender or number

Before-noun placement adjectives

As mentioned before, adjectives usually come after the noun in French. However, the word *usually* doesn't mean always, because in every language there are exceptions.

In French there is a group of adjectives that go before the noun. This is a group of the most common adjectives. It has been said that these adjectives often describe beauty, age, goodness, and size (acronym BAGS), but this is only a tendency and hopefully a helpful tool. Here is a list of some of the most common before-noun adjectives.

beau/bel: handsome (for masculine and masculine starting with a vowel) note: Beau in the plural is beaux

belle: beautiful (for feminine nouns)

joli(e): pretty

petit(e): small

grand(e): big

haut(e): high

gros, grosse: fat

jeune: young

long, longue: long

mauvais(e): bad

bon/bonne: good

pire : worst

vieux, vieille, vieil : old (Masculine, feminine, and masculine starting with vowel) nouveau, nouvelle, nouvel : new (There are three forms in the singular: masculine, feminine, and masculine used with words starting with a vowel. The masculine plural is *nouveaux*.

Examples

Une vieille dame   an old lady

Une bonne tarte   a good pie

La nouvelle voiture   the new car

What to do if there are two adjectives in a sentence?

If there are two adjectives, one before and one after, you can place them where they belong. In the phrase, une nouvelle voiture rouge.... A new red car, there is one adjective that will come before the noun, and another after.

If there are two adjectives that come before or two that come after the noun, use "et" (and) to connect them.

Examples

Une petite et belle femme   A small, beautiful woman

Une longue et mauvaise journée   A long, bad day

14B Translate the following phrases using the right adjective in the right place.

1. The red car

2. The pretty girl

3. The delicious pie

4. An old white house/ old white houses

5. The Italian lady

6. A nice neighbor (voisine)

7. A big family

8. A tall building

9. A green dress

10. The old, gray cat

11. Some mean dogs

12. The yellow papers

Chapter 15

This, These, His, and Hers
Demonstrative and Possessive Adjectives

There are two more types of adjectives you will learn in this chapter. You probably don't think of these words as adjectives, since both of them help us identify things we are talking about. They are indispensable, as you'll see.

Demonstrative Adjectives

In the sentence: "I really like this/that movie", the words **this** and **these,** as well as **that** and **those** are called demonstrative adjectives. They demonstrate which item you're talking about. With these words you'll be able to express this, that, these and those whenever you need to.

Je vois le film ce soir. I'm seeing the movie **this** evening. Here the word "ce" is this in the masculine singular form.

Ce, cet, and cette mean **this**. Ces means **these**.

Here are all the forms:

Ce: masculine singular

Ce manteau est trop grand. (This coat is too big.)

Cette: feminine singular

J'aime cette robe bleue. (I like this blue dress.)

Ces :   feminine or masculine plural

Elle va porter ces chaussures. (She's going to wear these shoes.)

69

Cet : masculine singular for nouns starting with a vowel

Louis veut venir cet après-midi. (Louis wants to come this afternoon.)

Note: If you want to say "that" and "those", use "là" after the nouns. Examples : cette robe-là (that dress) ces vélos-là (those bikes.) Là means "there ".

15A Add the correct form: ce, cette, ces, or cet

1. _____ voiture
2. _____ vélo
3. _____ amis
4. _____ matin
5. _____ idée
6. _____ garçon
7. _____ ordinateur (computer-masc.)
8. _____ portes
9. _____ insectes
10. _____ chaussettes

Possessive Adjectives

When you want to express who something belongs to, use possessive adjectives. It's the equivalent of saying his, her, your, our, and their.

The gender of the adjective is based on the object possessed, not the subject of the sentence (the owner of the object). Look at the following examples:

C'est mon stylo. (It's my pen.) Mon is the masculine form for "my". Masculine is used because a stylo is masculine.

Je vais à sa fête. (I'm going to her party.) Sa means her. Sa is the feminine form for her because fête is a feminine noun.

70

Singular possessive adjectives

	Masculine	Feminine	Plural
Je	mon	ma	mes
Tu	ton	ta	tes
Il, elle, on	son	sa	ses

Examples

Je donne **ma** clé à **mon** frère. (I am giving my key (f) to my brother (m).)

Elle apporte **ses** photos. (She is bringing her photos (f. pl).)

Donne-moi **ton** journal. (Give me your newspaper (m).)

Note: When you have a feminine noun that starts with a vowel, you'll still use the masculine possessive form, for the sake of pronunciation.

Example : Je vois mon amie Katie. (I see my friend Katie.) Use mon for either gender in the case of a vowel.

Plural possessive adjectives

In plural forms you only need to consider whether something is singular or plural, not its gender.

	Singular	Plural
Nous	notre	nos
Vous	votre	vos
Ils, elles	leur	leurs

71

Examples

Nous allons vendre **notre** maison. (We are going to sell our house.) House is singular, but it belongs to "us", nous.

Les voisins laissent **leur** chien dehors en hiver. (The neighbors leave their dog outside in winter.)

Vous mangez très vite **vos** repas. (You (plural) are eating your meals very fast.)

Note: Repas means meal, but doesn't need an s in the plural, because there is already an s. (This rule is true for words ending in s, z, and x.)

If you want to express possession without the pronoun (It's Fred's book), you can use "de", of. C'est le livre **de** Fred.

72

15B Complete the following with the correct possessive adjective.

1. My son _____ fils

2. Your (informal) cat _____ chat

3. Our opinion_____ avis

4. Their children _____ enfants

5. Her dress _____ robe

6. His boot _____ botte

7. His boots _____ bottes

8. My tomatoes _____ tomates

9. Our father _____ père

10. Their truck _____ camion

Chapter 16

Food and Restaurants

Aimer and Partitive Articles

One of the most useful regular verbs is **aimer**, which means to like or love. It is an ER verb so follows the normal pattern of other ER category verbs. The only tricky thing about this verb is perhaps the pronunciation, which is emm-ay for the infinitive.

j'aime	nous aimons
tu aimes	vous aimez
il, elle, on aime	ils, elles aiment

Use aimer to express liking a thing. Aimer with a person, however, expresses love. Use aimer bien to describe liking a friend. Sometimes people emphasize liking something a lot by saying, "j'adore ce film!" I love this movie!

Some languages don't permit you to love things, only people. In French you can do both, but context will help you know whether like or love is being used.

I like . . .

If you want to express that you like, love, or dislike something in general, you will use the definite articles, le, la, or les, before the noun. That expresses a general feeling about something.

Examples

J'aime le chocolat. (I like chocolate.) Je n'aime pas les chiens. (I don't like dogs.)

Il déteste la musique classique. (He hates classical music.)

Elle n'aime pas les olives. (She doesn't like olives.)

2-Verb Structure

You can also use aimer with a second verb like you would in English, as when you say I like to eat pizza. Like and to eat are 2 different verbs. Like in English, you'll only conjugate the first verb and leave the second verb in the infinitive.

J'aime partir à la plage. (I like going away to the beach.) Note that the verb partir stays in the infinitive.

Les filles aiment jouer dans le jardin. (The girls like to play in the yard.)

You'll see later on how you can use this 2-verb structure with many other verbs.

Partitive: Part of

If you want to express action involving a noun using verbs like to buy, to take, or to want, you'll use another kind of article, a partitive article. This expresses a *part* of something, instead of a general, universal statement about it. It's like saying *some* of something and is used with non-countable nouns such as wine or chocolate. It is also used with abstract nouns and ideas, like liberty or love.

You'll take into consideration the gender as you did with aimer but add the preposition **de**. Note that with countable nouns, like bananas, shoes, or cars, you'll still use the article **des**. Also, with containers, use an article, then the container name, then the word de (always used with any quantity or container). For example, un verre de jus. A glass of juice. Une carafe d'eau. A carafe/pitcher of water.

Partitive forms

Masculine form: du (de + le)

Je vais prendre **du** vin blanc. (I'm going to have some white wine.)

Feminine form: de la

Les Robert achètent **de la** viande pour leur grand repas de fête. (The Roberts are buying meat for their big holiday meal.)

Vowel form for both genders : de l':

Nous voulons **de l'**eau froide après le match. (We want some cold water after the match.)

Other examples

Elle voudrait du poisson et comme dessert, de la glace. (She would like some fish and for dessert, ice cream.)

Nous allons acheter des pommes pour la tarte aux pommes. (We're going to buy some apples for the apple pie.) Use des with countable nouns.

Cet homme veut trois bouteilles de vin rouge. (This man wants three bottles of red wine.) Use de after containers and quantities.

As you can see, the partitive lends itself well to foods. Later in this chapter you'll see this in action in a restaurant dialogue.

16 A Translate the following sentences, using the correct articles (partitive or not.) You can refer to the vocabulary on page 79.

1. I am going to buy some chicken.

2. He eats cake after every meal.

3. Jean-Luc likes pizza.

4. We have (prendre) milk with our cereal.

5. They are eating sandwiches for lunch.

6. I'll take cream in my coffee.

7. My cousins love eating ice cream in the summer.

8. She wants a Coke.

9. We'll take a carafe of water.

10. I'd like some white wine.

11. My mother is looking for some bananas and apples.

12. Sébastien is going to have some beer.

Restaurants in France

In France, restaurants generally don't open until about 7 pm for dinner or later. Some restaurants, especially in busy or touristy cities, may be open all day long. These restaurants will usually have a sign that reads "Service Continue", meaning they serve food all day long.

There will often be a special fixed menu giving 2 or 3 choices (appetizer, main course, and dessert, or two out of three) for one price. They call this le menu or menu prix fixe. What we call a menu in English the French call "une carte". This is related to our expression "à la carte".

When you arrive, you might get a carafe of water, though you usually have to ask for that. If you want bottled water, you'll order that by the brand name on the menu or just say *une bouteille d'eau*. If you don't want to pay for water, ask for une carafe d'eau. This is tap water, perfectly safe and often served chilled. (You normally cannot get ice cubes in Europe.) You'll order your food first, then your beverage (boisson). The "entrée" on a French menu is not the main course, as it is in the U.S. It is the appetizer, the "entrance" into the meal. The main course is "le plat principal" or just "le plat." Le Plat du Jour is the daily special.

At dinner, you will not be rushed through your meal. You can stay as long as you like, and you will have to request your bill when you're ready to leave. You do this by saying, "L'addition, s'il vous plaît."

Some Food Vocabulary

la soupe: soup

le vin: wine

la glace: ice cream

le gâteau: cake

la tarte: pie (au, aux for type)

la boisson: beverage

l'eau minerale: (pétillante/gazeuse ou plate)

le poisson: fish

la viande: red meat

le poulet: chicken

le lapin: rabbit

les raisins(m): grapes

le jambon: ham

le porc: pork

le Coca: Coke

le lait: milk

un légume: a vegetable

les fraises (f): strawberries

les pommes (f): apples

les champignons (m): mushrooms

la salade: salad, lettuce

le café: coffee

le jus de fruit: fruit juice

la crème: cream

le fromage: cheese

un œuf/ des œufs: an egg, eggs

la bière: beer

un demi: a half litre of wine or some other beverage

Restaurant terms

service continue: serving food all day

le menu/ la carte: a fixed menu, the regular menu

un apéritif: a type of before-dinner drink with alcohol

une carafe de: a carafe/pitcher of...

une assiette: a plate, a platter

un couteau, une fourchette, une cuillère: knife, fork, spoon

ouvert (e), fermé (e): open, closed

le serveur, la serveuse: waiter, waitress

gastronomique: a higher level of cuisine, gourmet

le petit déjeuner: breakfast

le déjeuner: lunch

un repas: a meal

nature: plain, as opposed to flavored; le yaourt nature is unflavored yogurt.

une carte bancaire: bank card

payer par carte bancaire: pay by card

l'espèce: cash   payer en espèce: pay in cash

Verbs for ordering food and beverages

vouloir (to want) je veux (I want) je voudrais (I would like)

prendre (to take) je prends (I'll take) nous prenons: (we'll take)

boire (to drink) je bois (I drink, I'll drink) nous buvons (we drink)

At the Restaurant   **Dialogue 3**

Serveur: Voici la carte et la carte des vins.

Client: Merci. Je vais regarder la carte.

              (Quelques minutes plus tard.)

Serveur: Vous êtes prêt(s) ?

Client: Oui. Je voudrais du poisson avec mélange de
              légumes.

Serveur: Qu'est-ce que vous voulez comme boisson ?

Client: Je prends du vin blanc.

Serveur: En bouteille ou en carafe ?

Client: En carafe. Un demi.

Serveur: Du poisson et une carafe de vin blanc.

Client: Oui, c'est ça.

Serveur: Très bien, monsieur/madame.

Additional vocabulary :

Prêt(e): ready

Plus tard: later

Qu'est-ce que vous voulez comme... : what kind of

Un demi: refers to a half-litre   Une bouteille: a bottle

TO DO: Create a dialogue of your own modeled after the one
above.

81

Chapter 17

How to Ask Questions

When you're in a new place and you want to find something, the ability to ask questions is indispensable! In this chapter you'll learn the general patterns for asking both yes/no questions and questions that seek specific information.

Yes/No Questions

There are 3 ways to ask yes/no questions in French.

1. Make a normal statement but give it the upward intonation at the end of the sentence. Tu viens avec nous? You're coming with us? This is generally used in informal situations among friends or family.

   Examples

   Vous avez des enfants? (Do you have children?)

   Il n'est pas prêt? (He isn't ready?)

2. A second way to ask a yes/no questions is to use a normal statement but put the question phrase "est-ce que" in front. This word seems long but is pronounced es-kuh. It is a multi-purpose question word that is similar to the English words do, does, is, or are. This form of question can be used in either a formal or informal context.

   Examples

   Est-ce que tu viens avec nous? (Are you coming with us ?)

   Est-ce que vous avez des enfants? (Do you have children ?)

Est-ce que tu achètes des tomates ? (Are you buying tomatoes?)

If you are ever stuck for how to ask a question, just fall back on est-ce que. The literal meaning is, "is it that . . ." This phrase is followed by normal word order.

3. The third method to ask a yes/no question is the inversion method, where the verb comes before the noun. This is often used in formal situations, but depending on the sentence, is sometimes the easiest form to use.

Examples

Avez-vous des enfants? (Do you have children?)

Vas-tu au supermarché? (Are you going to the supermarket?)

Ta mère, est-elle ici ? (Is your mother here?)

(Note that in the previous case the subject is presented first, then the inverted form with the pronoun given after. This is a common construction in French for a third-person subject, and there isn't a standard English equivalent.)

Notice that in this form, the verb comes before the subject. When you invert the verb and subject, you place a hyphen between the two. Avez-vous, sommes-nous, etc.

Be careful about translating directly from English. We use do and is/are a lot in our questions, but you won't necessarily do this in French for a similar question. Just translate the idea, not the actual words if they don't fit.

This form lends itself well to the *vous* usage in more formal speech.

17A Ask a question in French by translating the sentence into the 3 forms you just learned. Follow the example:

Example   Do they like their new house?

Intonation: Ils aiment leur nouvelle maison?

Est-ce que :   Est-ce qu'ils aiment leur nouvelle maison ?

Inversion :   Aiment-ils leur nouvelle maison ?

1.   Is Simone sick?

2.   Do you have a ticket? (un billet, formal)

3.   Do you like classical music? (informal)

4.   Are they coming to dinner?

5.   Are we late?

Information Questions

If you want information, you'll have to ask a different kind of question. In the yes/no question section you learned about 3 ways to ask a yes/no question. You can use method 2 and 3 to ask for specific information as well. Usually, though not always, you'll add a question word (how, why, when, who, etc.) to the phrase.

Here are some common question words:

how	comment
how much	combien (de)
who	qui
where	où
what	que or quoi (quoi is used after a preposition)
why	pourquoi
when	quand
which	quel, quelle (m/f)
which one	lequel, laquelle (m/f)

With **est-ce que**, you'll usually put the question word at the beginning of the sentence, then add est-ce que, then the rest of the sentence, keeping regular word order.

Examples

Quand est-ce que tu vas venir ce soir? (When are you going to come tonight?)

Pourquoi est-ce qu'elle est fâchée? (Why is she angry ?)

Combien est-ce que ça coûte ? (How much does this cost?)

Lequel est-ce que tu aimes? (Which one do you like?)

85

With the **inversion** method, you can use a question word in front of the inverted verb-subject.

Examples

Laquelle (feminine) aimez-vous? (Which one do you like?)

Quand vas-tu arriver ce soir? (When are you going to arrive tonight ?)

Pourquoi vont-ils partir si tôt? (Why are they going to leave so early ?)

Qui veux-tu inviter à la fête? (Who do you want to invite to the party ?)

With inversion, in the third person singular, sometimes a "t" is added to help in pronunciation when the verb ends in a vowel, as in the following examples:

Quand va-t-elle arriver ce soir? When is she going to arrive tonight?)

Pourquoi aime-t-il ce film ? (Why does he like this movie?)

You may notice that French people occasionally place the question word elsewhere in the sentence than at the beginning. This is common with informal usage. Once you are comfortable with all of the above methods you can try it yourself. Here are some examples:

Ça coûte combien? (How much does that cost?)

On va où? (Where are we going?)

Ils viennent chez toi combien de fois? (How many times do they come to your house?)

86

17B Fill the blank with the word or words that fit. (Comment, combien de, quand, où, pourquoi)

_____ pommes avez-vous ?

_____vas-tu arriver ? En train ou en voiture ?

_____ argent est-ce qu'ils ont ?

_____ vont-elles préparer le repas ?

_____ est-ce que vous avez peur ? (afraid)

_____ est-ce que tu joues des cuillères ? (spoons)

_____ vas-tu ?

_____ sont mes livres ?

_____ est-ce que vous parlez très fort ? (loudly)

_____est-ce que vous allez arriver ?

Finding Places

l'hôtel: hotel (m)   à peu près: approximately

le restaurant: restaurant   la cathédrale: cathedral

le bateau: boat   l'église: church (f)

le vélo: bike   la rivière: river

l'accueil: information or welcome desk (m)

devant: in front of   derrière: behind

à côté de: next to   près de: near to

87

loin de: far from

le coin: the corner

qui fait l'angle: makes an angle

le prix: the price

le tarif: the rate

par personne: per person

trouver: to find

se trouver: to be located

la rue: the road

la poste: the post office

la boîte aux lettres: mailbox

au bout de la/du: at the end of the...

le carrefour: the intersection

en face de: facing, across from

celui-ci: this one (masc) celui-là : that one (masc)

celle-ci: this one (fem) celle-là : that one (fem)

celles-ci, celles-là: these here, those there (feminine plural)

ceux-ci, ceux-là: these here, those there (masculine plural)

la gare: the train station

tout droit: straight ahead

à droite: to the right

à gauche: to the left

le forfait: package pricing

ensemble: together

le couloir: the hallway

tourner (à): turn (to the...)

déranger: to disturb

chercher: to look for

le feu: the stoplight

Asking for Directions   Dialogue 4

Ralph/Renée: Excusez-moi de vous déranger, monsieur.
                        Où est la poste la plus près d'ici, s'il
                        vous plaît ?

Monsieur: Il y a un bureau de poste à peu près cinq
                        minutes d'ici, dans la rue de la Liberté.

Ralph/Renée :   Où est la rue de la Liberté ? Là-bas, celle-
                        là ?

Monsieur: Non, elle est plus loin. Vous allez tout droit.
                        Ensuite vous tournez à gauche dans
                        l'avenue Emile Zola. La rue de la Liberté
                        est la première à droite. La Poste est en face
                        du supermarché. Il y a une fontaine juste
                        devant.

Ralph/Renée :   Merci, monsieur. Bonne journée.

Monsieur: Merci.

TO DO:

Create a dialogue of your own about finding a place,
modeled after the one above. Try to use some of the vocabulary
and new structures you have learned.

89

Chapter 18

Asking for Help

When you need help, remember how to ask questions (from the previous chapter). For simple medical needs, you can get a lot of help at a pharmacy, or for other needs, the police.

Here is some helpful vocabulary for health and emergencies.

Parts of the body

la tête: the head
la jambe: the leg
le cou: the neck
l'oreille: the ear (f)
la main: the hand
le genou: the knee
la dent : the tooth
les yeux: the eyes l'œil : an eye (m)
les doigts: the fingers (m)
l'estomac: the stomach (m)
le dos: the back
la colonne vertébrale : spine

le bras: the arm
le corps: the body
la bouche: the mouth
les cheveux: the hair (m)
le pied: the foot
les dents: the teeth
le nez: the nose
la chair: flesh
la gorge: the throat
l épaule: the shoulder (f)
le coeur: the heart
la peau : the skin

Verbs related to the body

respirer: to breathe
renifler: to sniff
digérer: to digest
goûter: to taste
toucher: to touch
se lever: stand up

sentir: to smell
avaler: to swallow
se reposer: to relax
bouger: to move around

90

Words Related to Health and Emergencies

Illnesses: Use *J'ai mal à* with a noun. Avoir mal à la... (f). Avoir mal au... (m). Avoir mal aux... (pl).

Examples: mal à la tête (headache), mal à la gorge (sore throat), mal à l'estomac (stomach ache), mal au genou (knee), mal aux dents (toothache), mal aux pieds (sore feet), mal aux jambes (sore legs.) J'ai mal **à** la tête. I have a headache.

J'ai **du mal à** + <u>verb</u> in the infinitive. J'ai du mal à respirer (I have trouble breathing.) Use this expression with a verb.

un rhume: a cold	une fièvre: a fever
une urgence: emergency	un comprimé: tablet (medication)
un/des medicament (s) : medication (s)	
la pharmacie: the pharmacy	la grippe: the flu
une blessure: a wound, injury	blesser: to injure
perdu(e): lost	volé(e): stolen voler : to steal
la police: the police	un bureau de police : police station

au seccours ! Help !

<u>Emergency Phone Numbers in France:</u>

Medical Help: Dial 15   Police: Dial 17

Fire: Dial 18

SOS Pan-Europe   Dial 112 (must have a SIM card in your phone)

Also, your hotel reception can be a resource for emergency help.

91

At the Pharmacy   **Dialogue 5**

Charlie: Bonjour, madame. Je suis malade. Peut-être vous pouvez m'aider.

Pharmacienne: Qu'est-ce qui ne va pas ?

Charlie :   J'ai mal à la tête et mal à l'estomac.

Pharmacienne: Avez-vous de la fièvre ?

Charlie: Non, je ne pense pas. Je mange et je bois trop.

Pharmacienne: Ah, bon. Prenez ces comprimés toutes les quatre heures et ne mangez que des choses légères pendant deux jours.

Charlie: Merci, madame.

Other expressions :

Qu'est-ce qui ne va pas?   What is wrong? What is the problem?

Aider: to help.   Est-ce que je peux vous aider? Puis-je vous aider? Can I help you?

Ah, bon : This can mean, oh, I see. Spoken in a questioning way it can mean, really?

Je ne pense pas   I don't think so.

     TO DO: Create a dialogue of your own modeled after the one above. Try to use some of the vocabulary and new structures you have learned.

92

Chapter 19

Regular -RE Verbs

This chapter will cover our last regular verb group, those ending in -RE. You have already seen some of these, like attendre, to wait or wait for. Let's look at the -RE conjugation with the word attendre.

j'attends	nous attendons
tu attends	vous attendez
Il, elle, on attend	ils, elles attendent

You'll see the stem, attend, followed by each appropriate ending. Some other -RE verbs conjugated like this are these:

perdre: to lose

vendre: to sell

rendre: to give something back

entendre: to hear

défendre: to defend

descendre: to descend, go down

Examples

Ils attendent devant le magasin. (They are waiting in front of the store.)

Olivier perd souvent ses lunettes. (Olivier often loses his glasses.)

93

Nous entendons le chien du voisin. (We hear the neighbor's dog.)

Je rends mes devoirs au professeur. (I am turning in my homework to the teacher.)

19A Take a moment and write down the conjugations of 3 of the above -RE verbs

1.   2.   3.

19B Translate the following sentences using the correct form of the -RE verb.

1.   We are waiting for the appointment (rendez-vous)

2.   You always lose your key.

3.   I hear the music from the neighbor.

4. He is returning the book to the library.

5. The boys defend their little brother at school.

6. They are selling the house at the beach.

Chapter 20

Numbers 31 to 60

In Chapter 7 you learned the French for number 1 through 30. That was a good start, and especially useful for dates. Now we'll go up to 60. The pattern of French numbers stays the same all the way to 69, when it will change. This will be covered in a later chapter.

You have seen that French numbers follow a predictable pattern, ten at a time. Then the pattern repeats. Beginning with twenty-one, you'll have the pattern vingt et un, with "et" included, but then the et is dropped until you reach trente et un, and so on.

This same pattern continues to sixty-nine. Look at the following pattern.

30	trente	40	quarante
31	trente et un/une	50	cinquante
32	trente-deux	60	soixante
33	trente-trois		
34	trente-quatre		
35	trente-cinq		
36	trente-six		
37	trente-sept		
38	trente-huit		
39	trente-neuf		

Use the same pattern you see above for the other numbers, quarante (40), cinquante (50), and soixante (60). Try to say them all aloud. Then say all of the numbers from one to 60.

Hotel Vocabulary

disponible: available

salle de bains: bathroom

l'accueil: welcome or information desk

coûter: to cost

prendre: to take

troisième étage: third floor   un étage : a floor

à côté de: next to

l'ascenseur : elevator (m)

un couloir: a hallway, corridor

je vous en prie: You're welcome (formal)

une clé: a key

une chambre d'hôte: a bed and breakfast

une auberge: an inn

une auberge de jeunesse: a youth hostel

Paul: Bonjour, mademoiselle. Avez-vous des chambres disponibles? J'ai besoin d'une chambre avec salle de bains.

Réceptionniste : J'ai une chambre au deuxième étage. Est-ce que cela vous convient ?

Paul :   Ça coûte combien la nuit ?

Réceptionniste : Ça coute 120 euros la nuit pour une personne. A quelle heure prenez-vous le petit déjeuner ?

Paul: Je le prends à 7h30, s'il vous plaît. Où est la salle à manger ?

Réceptionniste : Juste là, deuxième porte à gauche. Et quel est votre nom ?

Paul: Paul Dumont.

Réceptionniste : C'est enregistré, Monsieur Dumont. Voici votre clé.

Paul :   Est-ce qu'il y a un ascenseur ?

Réceptionniste: Mais oui, dans le couloir à côté de l'escalier.

Paul: Merci beaucoup.

Réceptionniste: Je vous en prie.

Chapter 21

Irregular Verbs

You have already learned three categories of regular verbs (-ER, -IR, and -RE), which follow predictable conjugations. You have also learned 3 irregular verbs so far, être, aller, and avoir.

Irregular verbs don't follow the typical rules for conjugation, although many times there will still be similarities. There are groups of irregular verbs that are conjugated in similar ways. It's a good idea to learn these groups of words together.

Many irregular words are among the most common you will use. This will make them easier to remember. Here are two common ones:

partir: to leave

je pars	nous partons
tu pars	vous partez
il, elle, on part	ils, elles partent

Here are some words conjugated like partir:

dormir: to sleep	mentir: to lie	sentir: to feel or smell
sortir: to go out	servir: to serve	repartir: to go out again

99

venir to come

je viens	nous venons
tu viens	vous venez
il, elle, on vient	ils, elles viennent

Here are some words conjugated like venir:

tenir: to hold	devenir: to become
soutenir: to support	revenir: to return
appartenir: to belong	obtenir: to obtain
maintenir: to maintain	

prendre: to take

This verb is often used when ordering food or buying things. Je prends means "I'll take..."

je prends	nous prenons
tu prends	vous prenez
il, elle, on prend	ils, elles prennent

Other words conjugated like prendre:

apprendre: to learn	comprendre: to understand
surprendre: to surprise	

mettre: to put, to put on (clothing or shoes)

je mets	nous mettons
tu mets	vous mettez
il, elle, on met	ils, elles mettent

100

Other words conjugated like mettre:

permettre (à): to permit   battre: to hit, to beat

combattre: to combat   promettre (à): to promise

(note: for permettre and promettre, use à before a person and de before an infinitive verb.)

More commonly-used irregular verbs

(Hint: the next 3 are conjugated alike)

écrire (à): to write, to write to

j'écris	nous écrivons
tu écris	vous écrivez
il, elle, on écrit	ils, elles écrivent

lire: to read

je lis	nous lisons
tu lis	vous lisez
il, elle, on lit	ils, elles lisent

dire: to say (à) to say, to say to

je dis	nous disons
tu dis	vous dites
il, elle, on dit	ils, elles disent

savoir: to know

je sais	nous savons
tu sais	vous savez
il, elle, on sait	ils, elles savent

voir: to see

je vois	nous voyons
tu vois	vous voyez
il, elle, on voit	ils, elles voient

Croire : to believe, is conjugated in a similar way to voir.

boire: to drink

je bois	nous buvons
tu bois	vous buvez
il, elle, on boit	ils, elles boivent

21A Study the irregular verbs above and try to conjugate 3 of them from memory. Tomorrow do 3 more from memory. Keep going until you have practiced all of them and similar verbs mentioned.

As you can see, many irregular verbs have other verbs conjugated in the same way. It's easier to learn them together in groups.

Tip: It's difficult to predict verb conjugations with new irregular verbs. A verb conjugation book is very helpful to have as a reference.

Chapter 22

Weather and Leisure

When you go on vacation, you'll likely have two questions: 1) What is the weather, and 2) What will we do there? In French, one irregular verb, "faire", is handy to provide expressions for these two situations. In addition, faire gives you a lot of phrases for other daily activities as well.

Faire: to make or to do

je fais	nous faisons
tu fais	vous faites
il, elle, on fait	ils, elles font

You can easily see why faire is an irregular verb. The conjugation is unusual, but the word is so common you won't have any trouble learning it. In the first, second, and third person singular, as well as the past participle, the pronunciation is the same. In English we have 2 words, make and do, for the one French word, faire.

Examples

Ma mère fait un gâteau chaque vendredi. (My mother makes a cake every Friday)

Comment faites-vous ce projet? (How are you doing this project?)

Qu'est-ce qu'on fait ce soir? (What are we doing this evening ?)

Je fais le ménage avant de partir. (I'm doing the housework before leaving.)

103

The verb faire is often used to describe or inquire about the weather.

Il fait beau aujourd'hui. (It's nice out today.)

Quel temps fait-il ? (What's the weather ?)

Il fait froid, il fait chaud. (It's cold out, it's hot out.)

Il fait du brouillard. (It's foggy out.)

Note: Some weather expressions don't use faire. Il neige: it's snowing. Il pleut: it's raining. (infinitives: neiger, pleuvoir)

22A Complete the following sentence with the correct form of faire. At the same time, observe some new expressions.

1. Nous _____ des efforts d'être à l'heure. (to be on time)

2. Ils _____ le jardinage le week-end.

3. Je _____ des erreurs quand je ne _____ pas attention.

4. Tu ne _____ pas assez de nourriture pour tout le monde.

5. Vous _____ trop souvent les courses.

6. Il va _____ beau cet après-midi.

104

Some Expressions with Faire

Expressions

- faire attention: to pay attention
- faire plaisir à: to please someone
- faire une erreur: to make an error
- faire une gaffe: to make a blunder
- faire la queue: to stand in line
- faire un voyage: to take a trip
- faire ses valises: to pack one's suitcases

Leisure expressions

- faire du camping: to go camping
- faire du sport : to play sports
- faire de la natation: to go swimming (as an activity; the verb "to swim" is nager)
- faire du shopping: to go shopping (leisure)
- faire une randonnée: to go hiking
- faire du cheval, faire de l'équitation: to go horseback riding
- faire une promenade: to go for a walk
- faire du ski: to go skiing

Note: Some team and certain other sports use the word jouer à (to play) instead of faire.

Expressions for daily tasks

- faire le ménage: to do housework
- faire les courses: to do errands, especially grocery shopping
- faire la vaisselle: to do dishes
- faire le linge: to do laundry
- faire la cuisine: to do the cooking
- faire le lit: to make the bed
- faire le repassage: to do ironing
- faire de la poussière: to do the dusting

il fait bon, il fait beau: it's nice weather, beautiful weather

il fait mauvais: It's bad weather

il fait froid, il fait chaud, il fait humide: It's cold, it's hot, it's humid

il pleut: It's raining Il pleut des cordes: It's raining cats and dogs

il neige: It's snowing

le brouillard: fog   la météo: the weather report (radio, TV)

le film: the movie, the film

une pièce de théâtre: a stage play

un billet: a ticket

faire un tour (à or en): take a walk, a drive, a spin (à or en is used with transportation. For example, Faire un tour à vélo, à pied, en voiture): take a short bike ride, take a short walk, ride in the car.

un concert: a concert

la pelouse: the lawn

la séance: a showing (repeated), such as for a movie

une brocante: a temporary flea market

quinze euros à l'heure (example): 15 Euros per hour

en plein air: in the open air, outside

si: if, so, or yes in response to a negative assertion

sinon: otherwise

C'est dommage: It's a shame, that's too bad

What to Do Today　　　　　　　　**Dialogue 7**

Mac:　　　Est-ce que tu sais le temps qu'il fait aujourd'hui?

Jan :　　　Non, pourquoi ?

Mac :　　　Nous avons besoin de choisir nos activités pour la journée. S'il fait beau nous pouvons aller au parc ou marcher dans le Marais.

Jan :　　　Ou bien, faire du shopping? Manger en plein air? Il y a beaucoup de choses à faire à Paris.

Mac :　　　S'il fait mauvais, nous pouvons aller voir un film ou une pièce, ou aller au musée.

Jan :　　　Oh, je voudrais voir une pièce de théâtre. Mais il faut trouver une pièce en anglais. Sinon, on ne comprend rien.

Mac :　　　(En regardant la météo à la télé)

　　　　　　Non, malheureusement, il pleut aujourd'hui. Et il fait froid.

Jan :　　　C'est dommage. Allons au Musée d'Orsay, alors, et puis allons voir un film après.

Mac :　　　Sous la pluie et le beau temps, on reste occupé à Paris !

Jan :　　　C'est bien vrai !

Additional vocabulary

malheureusement: unfortunately

sous: under　　　　　　　　　　c'est bien vrai! :　How true !

rester: to stay, to remain

Le Marais: a quaint neighborhood in central Paris

107

Chapter 23

Telling Time/ French Norms

Telling time in French has similarities with English. Once you learn the pattern and become familiar with the sound of the numbers, it will be easier to tell time in French.

There are two ways of telling time in France. One uses the regular time clock, and the other uses the 24-hour clock.

In Europe, the 24-hour clock is always used for any kind of scheduled event, such as a train departure, a movie showing, or store openings. If you are traveling in Europe, it is essential to be familiar with the 24-hour clock. If you don't know it by heart, carry a small chart or index card with the equivalents if you want to be on time for your train or anything else! In this chapter you'll learn about both.

Phrases:

Quelle heure est-il? What time is it?

Avez-vous l'heure ? Do you have the time?

Il est __(number)_____ heure(s) It is _____ (to give the time) Example: Il est onze heures cinq. (Five after eleven.)

In English we use o'clock when we give a time that is on the hour. In French, use the word "heure" (hour) for *all* times, regardless of what time it is, even if you are using the 24-hour clock. Refer to Chapters 7 and 20 for a review of numbers up to 60.

To give the time in French, you can use the number of minutes, just like you would in English.

You can add the phrases "du matin", in the morning, or "du soir", in the evening, if you are not using the 24-hour clock.

Examples

Il est trois heures. (It's three o'clock)

Il est huit heures vingt. (It's eight twenty; It's twenty past eight.)

Il est neuf heures quarante. (It's nine forty.) Pronounce the f like a v.

And so on.

For quarter after, you can say trois heures quinze (three fifteen) or use the expression Il est trois heures et quart. (It's a quarter past three.)

For half past, you can use the phrase "et demie". Il est trois heures et demie. It's three-thirty. It's half past three.

For a quarter to four, for example, use the expression "moins le quart", or minus a quarter. Il est quatre heures moins le quart. It's a quarter to four.

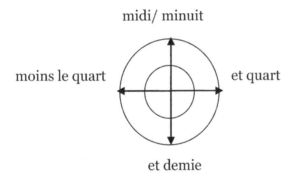

Noon is expressed by the word "midi". Midnight is "minuit".

Il est midi. Il est minuit. Il est midi trente.

Moins can also be used with numbers up to 30. For example, moins vingt (twenty till), moins cinq (five till).

109

For the 24-hour clock, use only the number of minutes, not the expressions, et quart, et demie, or moins le quart. Here are some examples of times using the 24-hour clock:

English form	French form	Spoken as:
8:25 am	8h25	Il est huit heures vingt-cinq.
9 :15 pm	21h15	Il est vingt et une heure quinze.
4 :30 pm	16h30	Il est seize heures trente.
11 :05 am	11h05	Il est onze heures cinq.
11 :40 pm	23h40	Il est vingt-trois heures quarante.
10 am	10h00	Il est dix heures.

French Norms for Time

Stores in France will typically be open following working hours, such as 9 to 5 or 6. However in larger cities, many stores such as grocery stores will have later closing times, even as late as 9 or 10. Almost NO stores will be open on Sundays, except some (not all) restaurants. Movie theatres, museums, and tourist sites should still be open on Sundays, though most museums will have a day during the week, often Monday or Tuesday, when they are closed.

Many small shops, such as hair salons, shoe repair, or small clothing boutiques and banks will be closed on Mondays, if they were open the previous Saturday. Smaller stores may also be closed during lunchtime for between one and two hours. This is almost always true for banks and sometimes for smaller grocery stores, especially in small towns. Often these smaller stores will also close for about three weeks in August.

Restaurants in both smaller towns and large cities typically close after the lunch hour, around 2:30 or 3 pm, then reopen at 7 pm. It is rare for restaurants to open for dinner before 7 pm, unless it serves the public all day. This will often be indicated on the window by the words "service continue."

For social gatherings it is not unusual for the French to be late by 10-30 minutes. This is known unofficially as l'heure française!

23A Write out the correct time. Use the normal time. (non-24-hour) Option: You can use phrases like "du matin" or "du soir" for clarity.

9:20 am

2:30 pm

4:45 pm

7:35 am

9:50 pm

12 noon

12:20 pm

23B Write out the correct time (in words) using the 24-hour clock. Also give the numerical short form (eg. 4h25)

4:40 pm

8 am

6:15 pm

11:30 am

9:30 pm

12 am

10 pm

Chapter 24

Numbers 61-100 and Dates

In Chapter 7 you learned about French numbers from 1 to 30. Then in Chapter 20 you learned 31 to 60. In this chapter you'll see number patterns to one hundred and beyond, and we'll look at how to express dates as well.

From 60 to 69, the same pattern that you have learned continues. Soixante et un, soixante-deux, and so on. However, at 70, the pattern changes. Observe the following:

70	soixante-dix	(Like saying sixty and ten)
71	soixante et onze	(Sixty and eleven ; like saying sixty plus eleven)
72	soixante-douze	(Sixty twelve)
73	soixante-treize	(Sixty thirteen) And so on.

When you reach 80, the pattern changes again.

80	quatre-vingts	(Like saying four-twenties Four times twenty)
81	quatre-vingt-un	(You drop the "et" for 81)
82	quatre-vingt-deux	And so on.

When you reach 90, the pattern looks similar to the shift between 60 and 70.

| 90 | quatre-vingt-dix | (four times twenty plus ten) |
| 91 | quatre-vingt-onze | (four times twenty plus eleven) |

100	cent
200	deux cents (straight 100s after 100 get an s)
350	trois cent cinquante
1000	mille (never gets an s in plural)
2000	deux mille
3500	trois mille cinq cents

24A Write out the French for the following numbers:

79	65
124	85
90	77
82	150
250	320

Dates

To express years, you can use the number and cent, followed by the rest of the number. For example, 1950 is expressed dix-neuf cent cinquante. You can also say mil neuf cent cinquante.

Examples

1445 quatorze cent quarante-cinq/mil quatre cent quarante-cinq

1205 douze cent cinq/ mil deux cent cinq

1876 dix-huit cent soixante-seize/ mil huit cent soixante-seize

2016 deux mille seize.

24 B Write out the French words for the following dates:

1824

1750

1200

1998

2005

1961

1599

1450

Chapter 25

Comparing Adjectives and Quantities

When you want to compare adjectives, like in the sentence, "he is richer than his brother," there is a simple formula you can use.

Look at the following examples:

Plus + adjective + que indicates *more than.*

Clarice est plus mince que sa sœur.   (Clarice is thinner than her sister.)

Moins + adjective + que indicates *less than.*

Frédéric est moins actif que ses parents. (Frédéric is less active than his parents.)

Aussi + adjective + que indicates *equality* in the adjective.

Elle est aussi belle que son amie. (She is as beautiful as her friend.)

Don't forget about agreement between the subject and the adjective for gender and number.

Pronunciation note: When you follow the word **plus** with an adjective, don't pronounce the final s, unless the adjective starts with a vowel. Example: Plus amusant: pronounce the s in a liaison. Moins amusant: pronounce the s in a liaison.

25A In the following sentences, place the best comparative in the blank. (Hint: Consult the chapter on adjectives (p. 60) if you need to review these.)

1. Le chat est (fatter than) _____ le chien.

2. Sallie est (less happy than) _____ Claire.

3. Nous sommes (as busy as) _____ nos enfants.

4. Les robes (dresses) sont (less expensive than)

   _____ les jupes. (skirts)

5. Ce vin est (drier than) _____ le champagne.

6. Cet examen est (less difficult than) _____ l'autre.

7. Ma mère est (less calm than) _____ mon père.

8. Tu es (as funny as) _____ ton ami.

117

25 B. Here is some more practice with comparing adjectives. Translate using the correct form of the comparative.

1. Adam is taller than Joe.

2. I am poorer (less rich) than my brother.

3. We are busier than our friends.

4. You are as intelligent as I am. (informal)

5. My dog is smaller than your cat.

6. Her car is as expensive as my house.

7. They are as interesting as you are. (plural)

8. You (plural) are less mean than you seem (sembler).

9. These films are more interesting than the books.

10. This road is less wide (large) than the avenue.

Good and Bad

For good and bad, there are irregular forms for *better* and *worse.*

bon/bonne: good   *meilleur (e):* better
                            (pronounced may-eur)

mauvais/mauvaise: bad   *pire* or *plus mauvais (e)* worse

Examples

Ce gâteau au chocolat est meilleur que le gâteau à la vanille. (This chocolate cake is better than the vanilla cake.) Note the masculine form of *better*.

La tarte est meilleure que le gâteau. (The pie is better than the cake.) Pie is feminine.

Le livre est pire (or plus mauvais) que le film. (The book is worse than the movie.)

The Best, the Worst (Superlatives with Adjectives)

To express the best or worst of something (also known as the superlative), as well as the prettiest, most intelligent, and so on, use the definite articles le, la, or les with the words meilleur(e) or plus mauvais(e)/pire.

For Good and Bad

Cette soupe est la meilleure de la semaine. (This soup is the best (soup) of the week.)

C'est le meilleur étudiant de la classe. (He's the best student in the class.)

Ce candidat est le pire pour le pays. (This candidate is the worst for the country.)

Cette décision est la plus mauvaise des choses. (This decision is the worst thing.)

For other adjectives

For other adjectives besides good and bad, there are 2 formats, depending on whether the adjective falls before or after the noun. Here are the patterns:

Adjectives before noun, (See page 66) keep the adjective before.

119

C'est le plus petit bateau ici. (It's the smallest boat here.)

C'est le plus jeune enfant du quartier. (This child is the youngest in the neighborhood.) Also: Cet enfant est le plus jeune du quartier.

Here are some examples where the adjective goes **after** the noun:

C'est l'élève la plus intelligente de la classe. (She is the most intelligent student in the class.) Note that in this form sometimes you will repeat the article.

François est le moins honnête de tous. (François is the least honest of everyone.)

Mes grands-parents sont les plus généreux de toute la famille. (My grandparents are the most generous of all the family.)

The article and adjective must both agree with the subject.

25C Translate the following sentences and supply the best superlative in each phrase.

1. This bike is the most expensive in the store.

2. He has the best collection of books. (la collection)

3. Ellen is the busiest of all of my friends.

4. This is the worst day of my life! (ma vie)

5. This film is the best of the festival. (le festival)

6. Madame Trudeau is the nicest teacher in the school.

120

Comparatives of quantity

To compare quantities, use the words plus de, moins de, and autant de. *Than* is still expressed by "que." You have seen the word *de* with other expressions of quantity.

Plus de + noun + que = more (quantity) than

Il y a plus de lait que de jus de fruit. (There is more milk than fruit juice.)

Moins de + noun + que = less (quantity) than

Brigitte mange moins de dessert que son frère. (Brigitte eats less dessert than her brother.)

Autant de + noun + que = as much as, the same quantity as (use instead of aussi que with expressions of equal quantity)

Les garçons ont autant de jetons que les filles. (The boys have as many tokens as the girls.)

More Examples

J'ai plus de temps que toi. (I have more time than you do.)

Mon père fait moins d'activités que ma mère. (My father does fewer activities than my mother does.)

Nous avons autant de vacances que nos collègues. (We have as much vacation time as our colleagues.)

Note: If you want to simply say "as much as", use "autant que." See the following example.

Vous avez autant que vos amis. (You have as much as your friends do.)

121

25D Supply the appropriate phrase for comparing quantities.

1. Ils ont _____ que moi. (more money)

2. Les voisins regardent _____ que nous. (fewer movies)

3. Nous buvons _____ que nos enfants. (as much wine)

4. J'en ai _____ que vous. (as much as)

5. Elle a_____ que sa sœur. (more clothes)

25E. More practice comparing quantities. Translate to French.

1. She drinks less water than I do.

2. Hope has less patience than her sister.

3. Evelyne eats fewer pastries than her husband.

4. We have less time than before. (qu'avant)

5. The children have fewer toys than last year. (l'année dernière

Chapter 26

Adverbs

Adverbs describe verbs, such as in the phrase "He talks slowly". Slowly is the adverb. In French, the adverb typically falls after the verb. An adverb can modify a verb, an adjective or another adverb.

Il va souvent au théâtre. (He goes *often* to the theater.)

Samuel court vite. (Samuel runs *fast*.)

Samuel court très vite. (Samuel runs *very* fast.)

Elle est trop maigre. (She is *too* skinny.) modifies adjective

Here are some common adverbs. You have already seen some of these in Chapter 11.

bien (well)   très (very)   mal (badly)

toujours (always)   trop (too much, too)   peu (little)

beaucoup (much, many)   vite (fast)

assez (rather, enough)

Many adverbs describe how often something happens, like rarely, often, sometimes, frequently, or never. Some adverbs involving time can be placed at the beginning of a sentence. A few adverbs, like heureusement and malheureusement (fortunately or unfortunately), or d'habitude (usually), will normally go at the beginning of a sentence.

d'habitude (usually)	demain (tomorrow)
hier (yesterday)	rarement (rarely)
souvent (often)	parfois (sometimes)
fréquemment (frequently)	quelquefois (sometimes)

Often an adjective can be made into an adverb simply by adding the ending –ment, the equivalent of –ly in English.

If the masculine form of the adjective ends in a consonant, the –ment is added to the feminine form of the adjective. Heureux becomes heureusement, for example. If a masculine adjective ends in a vowel, just add –ment.

Occasionally there is an addition of one or more letters when you add –ment. In the case of a masculine adjective ending in –ant or –ent, the ending will change to –amment or –emment, as in constant and constamment. Intelligent and intelligemment. Différent and différemment

Examples

constant.....constamment (constant...constantly)

vrai......vraiment (real, true...really)

évident.....évidemment (obvious...obviously)

exact.....exactement (exact, precise...exactly)

lent.....lentement (slow...slowly)

doux.....doucement (soft, gentle...softly, gently)

heureux.....heureusement (happy...fortunately, happily)

fréquent.....fréquemment (frequent...frequently)

franc.....franchement (frank...frankly)

absolu.....absolument (absolute...absolutely)

124

libre.....librement (free...freely)

poli.....poliment (polite...politely)

Sentence Examples

Il est constamment pressé. (He is constantly in a hurry.)

Je demande au professeur de parler lentement. (I ask the teacher to speak slowly)

Nous allons fréquemment à la plage en été. (We go frequently to the beach in summer.)

L'enfant répond poliment au voisin. (The child responds politely to the neighbor.)

26A. Create 10 new sentences of your own using adverbs from the above list.

1.

2.

3.

4.

5.

6.

7

8.

9.

10.

Chapter 27

Comparing Adverbs

When comparing adverbs, use the same format aswhen comparing adjectives (see page 116), using **plus, moins**, or **aussi** with the adverb + que. The difference is that the **verb** instead of the **adjective** is being compared. If you want to say *more* or *less*, use **moins que** or **plus que**. An *equal* comparison without an adverb (as much as) is **autant que**, (without the adverb), to say **as much as**.

Examples

Plus + adverb + que indicates **more than**:

Il mange plus vite que son frère. (He eats faster than his brother.)

Moins + adverb + que indicates **less than**:

Nous voyageons moins fréquemment que nos voisins. (We travel less frequently than our neighbors.)

Aussi + adverb + que indicates **equality**:

Annie parle aussi doucement que sa mère. (Annie speaks as softly as her mother.)

You can express simply more, less, or as much as using the same expressions:

Nous dormons moins que nos enfants. (We sleep less than our children do.)

Patrice étudie autant que sa cousine. (Patrice studies as much as his female cousin does.)

Better or Worse

If you want to say better or worse, as well as or as badly as, use the adverbs bien, mieux (well, better) or mal, pire or plus mal (badly, worse). Keep in mind these are adverbs and modify verbs.

bien: well   mal: badly

mieux: better   plus mal: worse

le mieux: the best   le plus mal: the worst

Note: Adverbs only have a masculine form.

Examples

Sandrine cuisine très bien. Sandrine cooks very well.

Je joue au tennis mieux que l'année dernière. I play tennis better than I did last year.

Benoît chante mal. Il chante plus mal que moi. Benoit sings badly. He sings worse than I do.

A different idea is expressed this way: Benoît chante moins bien que moi. Benoît doesn't sing as well as I do. Implication: Benoît sings fairly well, but I sing better than he does.

Il parle anglais moins bien que ses enfants. He doesn't speak English as well as his children do. (Literally: less well)

27A. Translate the following sentences using comparisons of adverbs.

1. Jeanne works less than Fred.

2. My friends dance more often than I do.

128

3. Christophe runs more slowly than Rémy.

4. Stéphane cooks as badly as his brother.

5. They travel less than I do.

6. I study as much as Jean-Marc

7. She talks more slowly than her mother.

8. We like to walk as much as you (plural).

Chapter 28

Traveling in France

France is one country where you'll never be bored. So many different experiences, regions, terrains, people, and foods await you. You also have many ways to get around this country the size of Texas, whether to large bustling cities or quaint medieval villages. In this chapter you'll see an overview of travel options as well as special travel vocabulary. A dialogue will illustrate travel vocabulary in context in a realistic travel situation. Helpful websites for each travel option listed here can be found in Appendix B.

Traveling by Train

Pros: There are pros and cons to traveling by train. Generally, train travel is fast, reasonable, efficient, and very pleasant. You can read or do other things while you travel, and you can usually get discounts if you reserve your tickets in advance. Taking a TGV is much faster than driving if you have a long distance to cover, for example, from Paris to Lyon. You can usually go from Paris to Provence in about four hours. It would take you nearly double that time to drive. TGV trains are ideal if you want to go from one large or mid-size city to another.

Cons: The main negative to train travel comes into play if you want to visit remote places or small towns. Some towns have limited access and not many trains per day, so you'll have to arrange your trip around the availability of trains.

TGV (high-speed) trains are not available for all cities.

SNCF is the company that will supply trains nearly everywhere the TGV doesn't go, except perhaps tiny villages, where you will probably have buses available. The SNCF is the national French rail company.

TER is similar to an SNCF type train, but it is regional.

- You can order tickets in advance online or at a train station. There are usually good discounts if you travel outside of peak times and get your ticket at least a month or two in advance.
- Reservations are required for TGV tickets (and are included in the price.) They are not required for other trains but recommended if you need a particular time slot or are traveling at a popular time (such as around French school vacations or weekend travel times, that is, Friday or Sunday evenings.)
  - Rail passes are also an option. The best companies are Eurail and France Rail. France Rail has better deals, especially if you are traveling with two or more people, with children, or a youth or a senior.
- See Appendix B for website addresses for SNCF, Eurail, and France Rail.

Traveling by Car

Pros: You will have easier access to remote places or smaller towns with a rental car. You can also share expenses if you have a family or several people with you. (Voiture de location: rental car)

Cons: The cost can be high for renting the car. Compare rental prices from the U.S. or your home country before you get there. You may get a better deal than in Europe. Tolls and gas are expensive. The time it takes is a factor, as is the fatigue of driving.

- In France there are autoroutes (blue signs), national routes (green signs), and departmental routes (yellow signs). Autoroutes are the fastest, but they have tolls except immediately surrounding cities. National routes generally follow the same paths but are longer and free.

- A few rules that are different than in the U.S.

  ➢ In France the right of way is to the person coming from the right, unless you see that they have a stop sign (look for a

131

thick, white line on the pavement, as well as the sign itself), a yield sign, or a light.

➢ If driving on the autoroute, stay on the right side unless you are passing.

➢ You cannot turn right on red or make U-turns in France.

➢ You cannot use your cell phone while you are driving.

➢ If you are in a town and don't see your destination, try the direction that says "toutes directions," or "all other directions." Usually this will take you back to main autoroutes. If you're coming into a town and want to reach the center, look for signs for "Centreville." Make sure you have plenty of gas before Sunday, just in case, especially in smaller towns, where stations might be closed. Also, speed limit signs are the numbers inside a red circle, and this is always kilometres (a kilometre is roughly half a mile).

➢ Special terms for driving: Péage: tolls/ Aire: rest stop, sometimes with food and gas/ Bouchon: traffic jam ahead/ Fluide: no traffic/ Sens unique: one-way (usually there's just an arrow on a sign).

➢ Whenever you see the word "interdit," that means "forbidden." If it's parking, driving, smoking, etc., don't do it if it says "interdit" or "défense de ..."

Traveling by Plane within France

Sometimes you can get someplace faster and as cheaply as by train, depending on your destination and the company you choose. Some low-cost companies are really no-frills, so don't be surprised by that. They still may be a very good deal.

See Appendix B for a list of no-frills and regular airlines that service French cities.

132

Traveling by Water In France

In recent years river cruises on barges or ships have become popular in France. In case you are wondering what waterways you could travel on, there are several. The Seine extends from Normandy to beyond Paris. The Saone and Rhone meet in Lyon, then the Rhone continues past Avignon and to the Mediterranean Sea. The Garonne and Gironde in the Bordeaux region, and the Rhine on the east side, near Strasbourg and flowing near Germany and Switzerland. In addition, there are some canals, like the Canal du Midi, some 150 miles in length, which meander through the idyllic valleys of Provence.

Typically, these cruises stop off at many villages and towns along the way and provide most meals on board (though not necessarily any entertainment). More information and websites are in Appendix B.

Helpful vocabulary for traveling

un guichet: a ticket window; also a bank service window or counter

un billet: a ticket (for métro or bus are called 'un ticket' tee-kay)

un couloir: an aisle or a hallway

une fenêtre: a window (seat)

un aller-retour: a round trip

un aller-simple: a one-way trip

le départ: the departure

l'arrivée: the arrival (f)

composter: to validate your (paper) train ticket prior to travel by punching it into a small machine (looks like a metal fence post, usually yellow or orange) at the station near the platforms.

une voiture de train: a train car is also called a voiture or wagon

133

une place: a seat (on a train, bus or plane) also seats at a performance (movie, play, opera, conference)

le retour: the return trip   la douane: customs

règler: to pay, to put into compliance; en règle: in compliance

une carte bancaire: a bank card (debit or credit)   espèce: cash

la gare routière: bus station (there is often one of these at train stations too, so you can get off the train and take a bus somewhere else.)

une auberge: an inn

un gîte: a bed and breakfast in someone's home

un camping, un terrain de camping: a campground

une caravan: a camping trailer

une auberge de jeunesse: youth hostel

un abri: a shelter

le TGV: the high speed train, bullet train (Train à Grande Vitesse)

une gare: a train station

une compagnie aérienne: an airline

un carnet: a book of 10 métro tickets

un ticket de métro: a single métro ticket

un quai: a train platform

les grandes lignes: Trains that go out to the rest of France

complet, complète: full

les horaires: the hours, the schedule

Buying a Train Ticket **Dialogue 8**

Phil s'approche du guichet à la Gare de Lyon pour acheter un billet de TGV. Il y a un agent au guichet qui donne des renseignements et vend des billets.

Agent: Bonjour, est-ce que je peux vous aider?

Phil : Oui, je voudrais un aller-retour, Paris-Lyon.

Agent : Vous voulez partir quel jour ?

Phil : Lundi, le 28 juin. Je préfère partir en matinée.

Agent : Et pour le retour ?

Phil : Je reviens le 5 juillet. Là, je peux partir l'après-midi.

Agent : En matinée le 28 ...j'ai un départ à huit heures et un autre à onze heures dix. A huit heures vous partez de la Gare de Lyon et vous arrivez à Lyon Part-Dieu à onze heures quarante. Le train qui part à onze heures dix arrive à quatorze heures cinquante.

Phil : Je prends le train de huit heures, s'il vous plaît.

Agent : Et les horaires pour le retour du 5 juillet?

Phil : Entre quatorze heures et seize heures, s'il vous plaît.

Agent : J'ai un train qui part à quatorze heures vingt et un autre à quinze heures quarante. Il y a moins de départs l'après-midi.

Phil : Je prends celui de quinze heures.

Agent : Vous arrivez à dix-huit heures quarante.

Phil : C'est parfait.

Agent : Première classe ou seconde?

135

Phil :   Seconde classe.

Agent :   Couloir ou fenêtre?

Phil :   Fenêtre, s'il vous plaît. Il y a une voiture qui vend de la nourriture ?

Agent :   Oui, il y a un wagon-restaurant.

(Il tape sur son clavier et imprime deux billets. Puis, il les montre à Phil.)

Agent :   Vous partez de la Gare de Lyon à huit heures et vous arrivez à onze heures quarante à Lyon Part-Dieu. Pour le retour vous partez le 5 juillet à quinze heures et vous arrivez à la Gare de Lyon à dix-huit heures quarante. Ce sera tout ?

Phil :   Oui, c'est tout. Merci.

Agent :   Ça vous fera deux cent soixante euros. Vous réglez comment?

Phil :   Par carte bancaire.

Additional vocabulary

des renseignements: some information

s'approcher de: to approach

aider: to help (aider à + verb: help someone do something)

la matinée: the whole morning

revenir: to come back

un clavier: keyboard

parfait(e): perfect

un écran: a screen

taper: to type

imprimer: to print

régler: to pay, to put into conformity

l'espèce: cash   en espèce: in cash, by cash

Note: see Chapter 20 for additional vocabulary for hotels and hotel reservations.

TO DO: Write a dialogue using some of the vocabulary and structures as the one you just read.

137

Chapter 29

Shopping in France

You will surely want—and need—to shop while you are in France. You may want to buy souvenirs, clothing, pastries, or you may need to pick up something you forgot to pack. You might wish to visit the open market and buy provisions for a picnic. You can't dispense with buying something. Knowing how to do it in French will make it that much more fun.

In this chapter you will read two dialogues. One takes place in a pastry shop (une pâtisserie) and the other in a clothing store (magasin de vêtements).

Vocabulary   **Shopping for Food**

désirer: to want, to desire

avoir l'air: to look, to seem

si: so, if; also "yes" in response to negative affirmation

venir de: to have just done something   Nous venons d'arriver (we just arrived)

un four: an oven

recommender: to recommend

une recommendation: a recommendation

un chausson aux pommes: apple turnover

la pâtisserie: pastry, pastry shop

sera: will be (future tense of être in 3rd person singular)

tenir: to hold; tenez, tiens can mean "here" or "here you are" when receiving something, such as change

la charcuterie: cold cuts, lunch meat

une boucherie: a butcher shop

la monnaie: change, coins

une livre de: a half-kilo (about a pound)

le marché: the open market, farmer's market

faire des achats: buy some things

un casse-croûte: a snack

un supermarché: a supermarket

la poissonnerie: fish market

la quinquaillerie: hardware store

les congelés: frozen foods

des produits de beauté: beauty products

le shampooing: shampoo

le dentifrice: toothpaste

une brosse à dents: a toothbrush

congé annuel: Annual closing of a store for summer vacation, usually July or August. Dates will usually be posted on the front door.

At the Bakery   **Dialogue 9**

(A la Boulangerie)

Boulangère: Bonjour, monsieur, madame. Vous désirez?

Sarah/Paul: Tout a l'air si bon ! Qu'est-ce que vous recommandez?

Boulangère: Nous venons de sortir ces chaussons aux pommes du four. Ils sont bien chauds. Et ici, il y a des croissants au beurre et des éclairs au chocolat et au café.

Sarah/Paul: Je prends deux croissants et un chausson aux pommes.

Boulangère: Très bien. Et avec ça?

Sarah/Paul: J'ai besoin de deux baguettes aussi, s'il vous plaît.

Boulangère: Bon, voilà. Deux croissants, un chausson aux pommes et deux baguettes. Ce sera tout?

Sarah/Paul: Oui, et pouvez-vous les mettre dans un sac?

Boulangère: Oui, bien sûr. Ça fait quatre euros cinquante, s'il vous plaît.

Sarah/Paul: Tenez. Merci, madame.

Boulangère: Je vous en prie.

Additional vocabulary

Ce sera tout? That will be all?

Pouvez-vous les mettre dans un sac ? Can you put them in a bag?

Ça fait: that makes . . . that comes to (for prices)

140

French Shopping Facts and Tips

- Most stores in France will have their hours posted on the front door using the 24-hour clock. Be sure to look because smaller boutiques and sometimes even grocery stores often close during lunchtime. This is especially true in smaller towns, where nearly everything will be closed during lunch. The hours will vary.

- In bigger cities, such as Paris, supermarkets are open fairly late, some (such as Monoprix) as late as 10 pm.

- Smaller stores run by one or just a few people, such as shoe repair, hair salons, and small boutiques, will usually be closed on Mondays, since they are likely to be open on Saturday. Many of these same smaller stores close for the entire month of August.

- If you need a haircut, don't plan to get one in France in August. Most salons are closed then for summer vacation.

- The 35-hour work week is the norm in France for non-management employees. This won't likely affect tourists, but it may explain why certain establishments don't have hours as long as you'd expect.

- Every town larger than a village will have a bakery and a pharmacy. The bakeries will have their days of closure on different days, so if one is closed, another one will be open. Most pharmacies will be closed on Sundays, but one in the area will be required to be open. This one is called the pharmacie de garde and its address will be posted on the door of the other pharmacies.

- Grocery stores are usually closed on Sundays. Plan ahead if you buy your own groceries during your visit. (Often there will be a marché available on Sundays.)

141

- Credit cards and debit cards are now widely accepted in France, except at the open markets. (Some individual merchants at markets may accept local bank cards.) You should have cash on hand for market shopping.

- Clothing is cut a bit smaller in France. This is especially true with the sizes S, M, L, and XL. Numerical sizes are more accurate. Either way, try them on to be on the safe side. See size equivalents later in this chapter.

un magasin de vêtements: a clothing store

mettre: to put, to put on

essayer: to try, to try on   une cabine d'essayage: fitting room

des vêtements: clothing (masculine)

une taille: a size

Je fais du trente-huit. I'm a size 38

une pointure: shoe size

une couleur: a color

un gilet: a cardigan   un pull, un pull-over: a sweater

aussi: also

un cadeau: a gift

quel, quelle: what, which (masculine and feminine)

une étiquette: a price tag, a label

celui-ci, celui-là: this one, that one masculine

celle-ci, celle-là : this one, that one feminine

ceux-ci, ceux-là: these here, those there (masculine)

celles-ci, celles-la: these here, those there (feminine)

comme: like, as ; sometimes used to ask what kind of

en solde, soldé: on sale, reduced

une robe: a dress

une jupe: a skirt

une chemise: a man's button-down shirt

une cravate: a tie

un pantalon, un jean: pants, jeans

des chaussures: shoes (feminine)

des chaussettes: socks (feminine)

un maillot de bain: a bathing suit, bathing trunks

un talon: the heel of a shoe

des bottes: boots (feminine)

un caleçon: leggings; also men's underwear (boxers)

une culotte: women's underpants   un slip: men's briefs

un soutien-gorge: a bra

une robe de chambre: a nightgown

un foulard: a scarf (accessory)

une écharpe: a winter scarf, a long fashion scarf

Household

une nappe: a tablecloth

des draps: sheets (masculine)

une serviette de bain: a bath towel

une serviette: a napkin

un set: a placemat

At the Clothing Store   **Dialogue 10**

(Au Magasin de Vêtements)

Vendeuse: Puis-je vous aider?

Marie/Joe: Bonjour, madame. Je cherche un pull-over
                  pour moi et aussi un gilet pour ma fille.
                  C'est un cadeau.

Vendeuse: Très bien. Vous les cherchez dans quelles
                  tailles?

Marie/Joe: Moi, je fais du trente-huit et ma fille fait du
                  trente.

Vendeuse: Vous préférez quelles couleurs?

Marie/Joe: Je ne sais pas. Voyons... voici des couleurs
                  claires. J'aimerais un pull comme
                  celui-ci. Combien est-ce que ça coûte?

                  (En regardant l'étiquette)

Vendeuse: Celui-là coûte quatre-vingts euros.

Marie/Joe: C'est un peu cher.

Vendeuse: Il y a des pulls et des gilets moins chers là, à
                  côté. Ils sont en solde cette semaine.

Marie/Joe: Merci, madame. Je vais les regarder.

TO DO: Write your own dialogue according to the model of
either dialogue 9 or 10.

145

French Clothing Size Equivalents

General Guidelines

Women's shoes			Women's clothing		
U.S.A.	*U.K.*	*France*	*U.S.A*	*U.K.*	*France*
6	4	37	6	8	36
6.5	4.5	38	8	10	38
7	5	39	10	12	40
7.5	5.5	39	12	14	42
8	6	40	14	16	44
8.5	6.5	41	16	18	46
9	7	42	18	20	48

Men's shoes			Men's Shirts		
U.S.A.	*U.K.*	*France*	*U.S,A*	*U.K.*	*France*
8	7.5	40	14	Same as US	36
8.5	8	41	14.5		37
9	8.5	42	15		38
9.5	9	43	15.5		39
10	9.5	44	16		40
10.5	10	45	16.5		41
			17		42

Chapter 30

Family Members and Relationships

In this chapter you'll learn some new vocabulary having to do with family members and relationships, as well as rooms and places in a home. Then you'll see a dialogue about a family gathering where you'll see that vocabulary in action.

During your visit to France, you may have an opportunity to talk about yourself, your family, and your life to people you meet. (Note: It may be helpful to review Chapter 15, possessive adjectives.)

Family and Home Vocabulary

la famille: the family

la mère: the mother	le père: the father
la fille: the daughter, the girl	le fils: the son
la grand-mère: the grandmother	le grand-père: grandfather
la tante: the aunt	l'oncle: the uncle
la sœur: the sister	le frère: the brother
la femme: the wife, the woman	le mari: the husband
la petite-fille: the granddaughter	le petit-fils: the grandson
la cousine: the female cousin	le cousin: the male cousin
une veuve: a widow	un veuf: a widower
célibataire: single	divorcé(e): divorced

marié(e): married   fiancé(e): engaged

un copain: friend, boyfriend   une copine: friend, girlfriend

ensemble: together

en retard: running late   en avance: early (adjective)

tôt: early (adverb)

ainsi que: as well as

Ça doit être... that must be...

en route: on the way

serrer la main de: to shake someone's hand

faire la bise: to give a French greeting, a light kiss on each cheek

se tutoyer: to use the "tu" informal form to address someone

J'y vais: I'll go, I'm going

quitter: to leave (requires a direct object, eg. leave the room)

sonner: to ring, to ring the doorbell

apporter: to bring something

la circulation: traffic

À table!: Come to the table! Time to eat!

House/apartment

la cuisine: the kitchen

la chambre :   the bedroom

le salon: the living room

148

la salle à manger:	the dining room
la salle de bains:	the bathroom
le couloir:	the hallway
l'entrée:	the entry, foyer
le placard:	the cupboard, closet
les toilettes (fem. pl):	small room in a home for the toilet; also, a public restroom
le garage:	the garage
le sous-sol:	the basement
le grenier:	the attic
le jardin:	the yard, garden
le balcon:	the balcony

A Family Gathering **Dialogue 11**

Bernard et Evelyne invitent leur fils, Rémi, sa nouvelle copine, Christelle, leur fille Sophie, son mari Stéphane, et leurs enfants, à manger chez eux un dimanche après-midi. Les grands-parents viennent aussi.

Bernard: Quelqu'un sonne. J'y vais.

Evelyne: Sophie et Stéphane viennent un peu en retard. Ils sont en route. Ça doit être Rémi, alors.

Bernard: (Il ouvre la porte.) Salut, Rémi. Tu vas bien?

Rémi: Pas mal. Il y a beaucoup de circulation aujourd'hui. Tiens, j'ai apporté du vin. Christelle a un gâteau.

Bernard: Merci. Ça a l'air bon. (Une jeune fille arrive.) Bonjour, tu dois être Christelle.

Rémi: Papa, je te présente ma copine, Christelle.

Bernard: Enchanté, Christelle. Bienvenue chez nous.

Christelle: Merci.

(Les grands-parents arrivent au même temps.)

Evelyne: Bonjour, Christelle. Je te présente ma mère, la grand-mère de Rémi, Madame Foucoult. Et voici Monsieur Foucoult.

Monsieur F: Je suis le grand-père !

Christelle: Je suis heureuse de faire votre connaissance. (Elle serre la main de chaque personne) Evelyne, votre repas sent très bon !

150

Evelyne: Tu peux me tutoyer, Christelle.

Bernard: Voici Sophie qui arrive avec sa famille. (Sophie et sa famille arrivent. Tout le monde s'embrasse.)

Evelyne: C'est Christelle, la copine de Rémi. Christelle, c'est ma fille Sophie, son mari Stéphane et leurs enfants, Maxime et Chloé. Et voici le chien de Maxime. Il s'appelle Lilo. Maxime ne quitte pas la maison sans Lilo.

Bernard: Je suis sûr que tout le monde a faim!

Evelyne: Je vous sers l'apéritif. Et après, à table!

Some phrases for polite conversations

J'ai (numéro) enfants. I have (number) children.

J'habite à/au/ en   I live in (à for cities, en or au for countries)

Je viens de...   I come from...

Est-ce que vous habitez ici depuis longtemps? Have you lived here for a long time? (You can use this phrase with other verbs as well.)

Est-ce que vous faites ce travail depuis longtemps ? Have you done this work for a long time?

Est-ce que vous avez des enfants? Do you have children?

Qu'est-ce que vous faites/ Quelle est votre profession ? What do you do? What is your profession?

   (Note: the French are not as quick to speak of jobs and careers as are Americans, who identify more with their work. Try to ask other questions first. Never ask about income or anything that would hint at this.)

151

Chapter 31

Direct Object Pronouns

If we didn't have pronouns, we would be repeating ourselves all the time. Imagine saying this: "I went to the store for some tomatoes, but the store was out of tomatoes, so I don't have any tomatoes for the salad tonight." Pronouns help us to avoid repeating ourselves.

In French, a direct object pronoun in third person is simply **le**, **la**, or **les** (just like the articles). The pronoun you choose, as you might guess, depends on whether the pronoun represents a noun that is **masculine, feminine, or plural**. They come before the verb that acts upon them. Look at the following examples.

Il y a beaucoup d'oiseaux dans le jardin. Je **les** vois tous les matins.

There are many birds in the garden. I see **them** every morning.

Ma cousine vient demain matin. Je vais **la** chercher à l'aéroport.

My (female) cousin is coming tomorrow morning. I'm going to pick **her** up at the airport.

Ton livre est sur la table. Veux-tu **le** prendre? Your book is on the table. Do you want to take it?

•   When you have a verb that starts with a vowel, you'll use the apostrophe, like you do with articles.

A ce restaurant le poisson est très bon. Je **l'**aime beaucoup.

At this restaurant, the fish is very good. I like it a lot.

152

- If there are two verbs, place the pronoun in front of the verb that acts upon it.

Elle adore cette robe. Elle veut l'acheter. She loves this dress. She wants to buy **it**.

- In the case of an imperative, the pronoun goes after the verb. This is the only time the pronoun changes places. It's then connected by a hyphen. In the negative imperative, however, begin the sentence with *ne* and keep the pronoun before the verb, as usual.

J'achète le journal chaque semaine. Prends-**le**. (Prends is the tu form of prendre, to take) Prenez-**le**. (Prenez is the Vous form) I buy the newspaper every week. Take **it**.

Ces pommes sont trop chères. Ne **les** achète pas. These apples are too expensive. Don't buy **them**.

(Note: In the tu form of -ER verbs, drop the s in the imperative.)

31A In the following sentences, use the correct direct object pronoun in the third person singular or plural.

1. Je descends la valise. Je _____ descends.

2. Nous cherchons l'adresse. Est-ce que tu _____ sais?

3. Il y a des chiens mignons dans le parc. Vous _____ voyez ?

4. Ces gâteaux ont l'air bons, mais je ne _____ achète pas.

5. Mon professeur n'est pas gentil. Je ne ____ aime pas.

6. Voici la clé. Prenez-_____ !

7. Vos bottes (boots) sont sales. Ne _____ mettez pas à l'intérieur.

153

8. Le vélo est dans le garage, mais je ne _____ trouve pas.

When you are referring to people using the first and second person, singular and plural, you'll use the same placement as for the third person, but with different pronouns. Some of the pronouns look familiar since they are used grammatically in other ways.

je: me, m'   nous: nous

tu: te, t'   vous: vous

il, elle: le, la, l'   ils, elles : les

Examples

Les voisins **nous** invitent pour dimanche soir. The neighbors are inviting **us** for Sunday evening.

Il ne **me** regarde même pas. He doesn't even look at **me**.

Je **vous** présente mon collègue, George. (In an introduction) This is my colleague, George. (Literally: I present to **you** my colleague, George.)

31B. Translate the following sentences, using the correct pronoun referring to people.

1. Are you listening to me?

2. My neighbors are nice. I see them in their garden each afternoon.

154

3. Your parents are looking for you.

4. The (female) dancer (danseuse) is very good. I like to watch her.

5. I invite you (plural) to my house this weekend.

6. She's calling her friends now. She calls them often.

7. My grandfather takes us to the countryside each summer.

8. My sister is waiting for me in front of the church.

Chapter 32

Indirect Object Pronouns

An indirect object pronoun will always be a person. The verb you use normally has to do with communication or transfer of physical goods. In other words, verbs like talk, say, explain to, and ask will be in the communication category. Verbs like give, loan, borrow, and buy for someone are in the category of transfer of goods. The indirect object pronouns for je, te, nous, and vous are the same as for the direct object pronouns. Only il, elle, ils, and elles have different forms.

When there is a noun *instead* of an indirect object pronoun, this is introduced by the preposition à.

For example, J'écris **à** mon fiancé tous les jours.

(I write **to** my fiancé every day.)

Elle donne un nouveau manteau **à** son frère. (She is giving (**to**) her brother a new coat.)

Verbs of communication:

demander à: to ask	dire: to tell
écrire à: to write	expliquer: to explain
montrer à: to show	parler: to speak
téléphoner à: to phone	répondre: to respond
sourire à: to smile at	plaire à: to please someone

156

<u>Verbs of Transfer:</u>

acheter à: to buy (for someone)   apporter à: to bring

donner à: to give   emprunter à: to borrow

offrir à: to give (a gift)   prêter à: to lend

remettre à: to turn in, hand in   rendre à: to give back

envoyer à: to send

<u>The Indirect Object Pronouns</u>

je: me   nous: nous

tu: te   vous: vous

il, elle: lui   ils, elles: leur

Examples

Je lui dis qu'on va partir. (I am telling him that we're going to leave.)

Elle lui achète un cadeau d'anniversaire. (She's buying him a birthday gift.)

Nous leur prêtons notre voiture. (We're loaning them our car.)

Il nous dit la vérité. (He's telling us the truth.)

157

32 A Complete the following sentences using the correct indirect pronoun.

1. She gives him the letter. Elle _____ donne la lettre.

2. Olivier is buying her a new car. Olivier _____ achète une nouvelle voiture.

3. The director gives us the answer. Le directeur _____ donne la réponse.

4. They will explain to you (formal) the process. Ils _____ expliquent le processus.

5. The committee is going to answer me tomorrow. Le comité va _____ répondre demain.

6. He writes to her often. Il _____ écrit souvent.

7. We are giving them an answer next week. Nous _____ répondons la semaine prochaine.

8. I'll give you (informal) the keys now. Je _____ donne les clés maintenant.

158

Chapter 33

Expressing Desires, Possibilities, and Obligations

In this chapter you will learn how to express desires and preferences using the verbs *préférer* and *vouloir*. You'll use the verb *devoir* to express obligation, and *pouvoir* to express ability or possibility. Three out of the four new verbs are irregular, but they are conjugated in a similar way. All of them must be used in combination with other verbs to say things like, "I prefer to see a film", or "You have to sleep now." (Exception: when using devoir for "to owe," you don't need another verb.)

Préférer is a regular verb, so we'll start there. The only unusual thing about préférer is that it changes accents in all except the nous and vous forms. If you listen to the difference in the "e" between préférer and préfère, you'll hear why the accent must change.

je préfère	nous préférons
tu préfères	vous préférez
il, elle, on préfère	ils, elles préfèrent

As in English, you can follow préférer with a second verb. You don't need to add any prepositions between the two verbs, and you will not conjugate the second verb.

Je préfère aller au musée. (I prefer to go to the museum.)

Nous préférons rester à l'hôtel ce soir. (We prefer to stay at the hotel this evening.)

159

- You can also follow préférer with a noun:

Ils préfèrent ce film. (They prefer this film.)

- The easiest way to use préférer is to follow it with a verb or a noun, as in the above examples. (If you introduce a new subject, for example, I prefer that **he** come with us..., you will need to use a different verb tense, the subjunctive, which you haven't yet studied.)

vouloir – to want

A stronger way to express desire is to use the word *vouloir*, to want. It is an irregular verb. The singular forms are all pronounced the same way.

je veux	nous voulons
tu veux	vous voulez
il, elle, on veut	ils, elles veulent

Ils veulent partir en avance. (They want to leave early.)

Nous voulons manger au restaurant indien au coin. (We want to eat at the Indian restaurant on the corner.)

Qu'est-ce que vous voulez boire ? (What do you want to drink?)

Je veux te voir. (I want to see you.)

- If you are ordering or requesting something at a restaurant or store, it is more polite to use the conditional form, I would like, or je voudrais.

Je voudrais le plat du jour, s'il vous plaît. (I would like the special of the day, please.)

160

pouvoir – to be able to

To express the ability or possibility to do something you can use the irregular verb *pouvoir*, to be able to. Notice the similarity in the conjugation with vouloir. The singular forms are pronounced alike, as for vouloir.

je peux	nous pouvons
tu peux	vous pouvez
il, elle, on peut	ils, elles peuvent

Il peut nous appeler cet après-midi. (He can call us this afternoon.)

Vous pouvez venir avec nous. (You can come with us.)

Nous pouvons louer des vélos dans ce magasin. (We can rent bikes in this store.)

Je peux faire la vaisselle et le linge. (I can do the dishes and the laundry.)

devoir – to have to, to owe

The last verb to be covered in this chapter is devoir. This means to have to, must, or to owe something. The singular forms are pronounced alike.

je dois	nous devons
tu dois	vous devez
il, elle, on doit	ils, elles doivent

Je dois aller chez le dentiste à quatorze heures. (I have to go to the dentist at two o'clock.)

161

Tu me dois cinquante euros. (You owe me fifty Euros.)

Nous devons partir à l'heure. (We need to leave on time.)

Vous devez venir plus tôt la prochaine fois. (You must come earlier the next time.)

- The word devoir is also a noun. In the singular, devoir means duty. In the plural, les devoirs, it means homework. Les enfants font leurs devoirs. (The children are doing their homework.)

- You can also use the word devoir in *to owe* with a non-number.

  Je te dois un service. (I owe you a favor.)

33A Complete the following sentences using the best choice : préférer, devoir, pouvoir, or vouloir. (Sometimes more than one will fit.)

1. De notre chambre d'hôtel, nous _____ voir les montagnes.

2. Les garçons _____ finir leurs devoirs avant de sortir.

3. Si tu _____, je _____ faire le repas.

4. Mon frère _____ voir le nouveau film de Spielberg.

5. Je ne _____ pas déjeuner avec toi demain. Je _____ aller chez le coiffeur.

6. Les filles _____ voir le film avec nous.

7. Est-ce que vous _____ prendre un dessert ?

8. Vous ne _____ pas vous garer (park) ici. C'est interdit.

9. Attendez, je vous _____ de l'argent.

10. Qu'est-ce que vous _____ faire ce soir ?

Too Busy...Trop Occupé   Dialogue 12

La mère de Fabien est dans la cuisine en train de préparer le petit déjeuner à la famille.

Fabien: Maman, je veux aller chez Christophe. Il a de nouveaux jouets qu'il a reçus pour son anniversaire.

Mère: Non, Fabien, tu dois finir tes devoirs. Après, tu peux aller chez Christophe.

Fabien: Je peux les faire cet après-midi.

Mère: Non, cet après-midi nous devons aller voir ta tante Mimi.

Fabien: Ce soir, alors. Je finis mes devoirs ce soir.

Mère: Ne veux-tu pas regarder de film à la télé avec nous ce soir ? Nous voulons commander une pizza.

Fabien: (Il hésite) Je préfère finir mes devoirs demain. Demain est dimanche.

Mère: D'accord. Demain matin on doit aller à l'église. Tu peux les faire après le déjeuner. Demain soir nous pouvons aller voir la nouvelle exposition au musée d'art.

Fabien: Le musée ? Je préfère faire mes devoirs.

164

Additional vocabulary

Maman: Mom, Mommy, Mother

en train de + verb: in the process of

hésiter: to hesitate   hésiter à + verb: hesitate to do something

un jouet: a toy

un jeu vidéo: a video game

commander: to order

TO DO: Write a dialogue after the model above, using devoir,

pouvoir, vouloir and préférer.

Chapter 34

The Past Tense with Avoir

In French, the normal past tense, which expresses events that have been completed, is called the passé composé. The word composé is like our word "compound." The passé composé is a compound tense, which means it has two parts.

To form the passé composé for most verbs, you will create the first part (called an auxiliary, or helping verb), which is simply the present tense conjugation of <u>avoir</u>. Then for the second part you will add a past participle (a special form for the past), which stays the same. Each of the three regular verb categories has its own form of the past participle, as you will see. Each individual irregular verb has its own past participle.

-ER Verbs

Let's look at an example using the word *manger*, to eat. You'll see the pattern for the -ER verb category. All past participles of -ER verbs are formed the same way.

j'ai mangé	nous avons mangé
tu as mangé	vous avez mangé
il, elle, on a mangé	ils, elles ont mangé

Examples of -ER past tense sentences

On a trouvé la bonne adresse. (We found the right address.) *trouver*

Chantal et moi avons marché toute la matinée. (Chantal and I walked all morning.) *marcher*

Vous avez pensé la même chose que moi. (You thought the same thing as I did.) *penser*

Hier j'ai acheté une nouvelle jupe. (Yesterday I bought a new skirt.) *acheter*

- If you have a direct or indirect object pronoun, this word goes before the first part (auxiliary). J'ai vu mon frere. Je l'ai vu.

- The verb agrees with a preceding direct object, though in most cases you won't hear the difference. You will have to write it, however.

Example

J'ai vu ta voiture. Je l'ai vue. Mes parents: Je les ai vus.

- No agreement is needed with indirect object pronouns.

- In the case of negatives, the ne and pas go around the auxiliary.

Example
- Je n'ai pas vu le journal. (I didn't see the newspaper.)
- Note : Place adverbs after the auxiliary, unless they are very long: Il a souvent écrit à sa mère. Nous avons marché lentement.

-IR Verbs

Let's see how this works with -IR category regular verbs, using the word choisir. Each past participle for –IR words ends in **i**.

j'ai choisi	nous avons choisi
tu as choisi	vous avez choisi
il, elle, on a choisi	ils, elles ont choisi

167

Examples of -IR past tense sentences

Bernard a fini sa thèse. (Bernard finished his report.) *finir*

Nous avons rempli les papiers. (We filled out the papers.) *remplir*

J'ai réfléchi à ton idée. (I thought about/reflected on your idea.) *réfléchir à.*

-RE Verbs

Lastly, we have the 3rd category of regular verbs, the **-RE** verbs. The past participle is different from the other two categories. It ends in **u**. See this below with the verb perdre, to lose.

j'ai perdu	nous avons perdu
tu as perdu	vous avez perdu
il, elle, on a perdu	ils, elles ont perdu

Examples of -RE past tense sentences

Frédéric a rendu ses livres à la bibliothèque. (Frédéric turned in his books to the library.) *rendre*

Ils ont attendu pendant une heure. (They waited for an hour.) *attendre*

J'ai entendu le bruit à côté. (I heard the noise next door.) *entendre*

Les voisins ont vendu leur maison à la plage. (The neighbors sold their beach house.) vendre

34A Complete the sentences with the verb in the parentheses in the past tense

1. Mes sœurs _____ (déjeuner) chez notre tante.

2. Joey _____ (attendre) ses amis devant le cinéma.

3. Nous _____ (jouer à) cartes jusqu'à (until) minuit.

4. Tu _____ (aimer) ton cadeau.

5. Elle _____ la bouteille. (remplir)

6. Vous _____ (parler) du problème.

7. J' _____ (chercher) tes chaussures mais je _____ (ne...rien trouver).

8. Tu _____ ton projet ? (finir)

9. Hier matin, Jean-Michel _____ (travailler) dans le jardin.

10. Ils _____ (rendre) leurs devoirs en avance.

Irregular Verbs

Here are some past participles for common irregular verbs:

voir: vu   (see)   boire : bu   (drink)

être: été   savoir : su   (to know facts, awareness)

169

avoir: eu	connaître: connu (to have deeper knowledge of, experience with)
devoir: dû	pouvoir: pu
vouloir: voulu	ouvrir: ouvert (open)
faire: fait	écrire: écrit (write)

Examples

Sophie a fait la vaisselle. (Sophie did the dishes.)

Les garçons ont bu tout le lait. (The boys drank all the milk.)

J'ai dû partir pour prendre le train. (I had to leave to catch the train.)

As-tu connu ma copine au lycée ? (Did you know my girlfriend in high school?)

Nous avons vu le journal ce matin. (We saw the newspaper this morning.)

34B Translate the following sentences using irregular verbs.

1. We had some problems with the car.

2. I was in Chicago last weekend.

3. Did you (plural) drink all of the red wine?

4. Lionel saw some children in the street.

5. I was able to finish my program in six months.

6. Thierry wanted to come with us to the movie but he had to work.

34 C Translate the following sentences into French. Verbs will be both regular and irregular.

1. We bought some shoes last weekend.

2. The restaurant served lunch until (jusqu'à) two o'clock.

3. Yesterday my friend lost his keys.

4. His children were able to visit the hospital.

5. Saturday night Alice slept in the yard.

6. I saw the film three times (fois).

7. We drank a lot of water after the tennis match. (match de tennis)

8. He knew this boy in high school.

Chapter 35

Past Tense with Etre

As you learned in the previous chapter, most verbs are formed using the verb avoir with a past participle. Not all verbs are formed this way, however. There are other *specific* verbs that use être instead of avoir. These tend to be verbs of motion or change of state. They will be formed in the same way, but with the present tense of the verb être (instead of avoir) as the auxiliary, plus the past participle of the verb.

• Although these verbs tend to be verbs of motion, not all verbs of motion will use être in the past tense. Quite a few do not.

• When using être, you'll have to have agreement between the past participle and the subject. (You'll see a few examples of this in the following list.)

The most common verbs conjugated with être

aller	(to go)	Tu es allé au restaurant ce week-end?
arriver	(to arrive)	Je suis arrivé en ville vers 10 heures du matin.
venir	(to come)	Paul est venu avec nous faire un pique-nique.
revenir	(to come back)	Françoise est revenue au bureau hier matin.
devenir	(to become)	Vous êtes devenu chef.
entrer	(to enter)	Chantal est entrée dans le magasin.

rentrer	(to return home)	Nous sommes rentrés tard après le travail.
retourner	(to go back)	Les sœurs sont retournées en France pour la troisième fois.
partir	(to leave)	Vous êtes partis ensemble à Lyon ?
sortir	(to go out)	Bertrand est sorti avec Juliette voir un concert.
passer	(to go by)	On est passé chez toi hier.
rester	(to stay)	Mes parents sont restés chez eux tout l'après-midi.
tomber	(to fall)	Sa grand-mère est tombée dans le supermarché.
monter	(to go up)	Lucie est montée dans sa chambre.
descendre	(to go down)	On est descendu dîner en ville.
naître	(to be born)	La petite fille est née en 1988.
mourir	(to die)	Mon voisin est mort l'été dernier. (feminine, morte)

- The verbs sortir, passer, monter, and descendre are able to take direct objects, and that changes the meaning. Sortir normally means to go out, but if used with a direct object, it means to take something out, in which case you'll use the avoir auxiliary instead. Here are some examples of this exception:

J'ai sorti le chat ce matin. (I put the cat outside this morning.)

Marianne a descendu la valise du grenier. (Marianne brought down the suitcase from the attic.)

Nous avons monté les décorations de Noël au deuxième étage. (We took the Christmas decorations up to the second floor.)

J'ai passé l'été en Provence. (I spent the summer in Provence.)

- With inverted questions, the auxiliary goes first followed by the subject pronoun (vous, etc), then the past participle.

Avez-vous trouvé vos clés? (Have you found your keys?)

35A Supply the following sentences with the correct form of the verb in parentheses (including the auxiliary):

1. Joël _____ au stade avec son frère. (aller)

2. Nous _____ dans le restaurant. (entrer)

3. Ma grand-mère _____ en 1920. (naître)

4. L'homme _____ du taxi. (descendre)

5. Les filles _____ avec leurs amies à la fête. (sortir)

6. Quand _____ vous _____ ? (arriver)

7. Marion _____ chez moi tres tôt ce matin. (passer)

8. Leurs cousins _____ des vacances dimanche soir. (revenir)

35B Now do the same thing as above, but some verbs will use avoir while others will use être.

1. Nous _____(passer) au magasin et nous _____(acheter) du lait.

174

2. Le weekend dernier, mes voisins du quartier

   _____ (manger) ensemble.

3. Ce matin, je _____(sortir) la poubelle
   (trashcan).

4. L'été dernier ma famille _____ (aller) en
   Grèce.

5. Esther _____ (tomber) dans l'escalier.

6. Ces gens _____ (vouloir) aller avant
   nous.

7. Pendant le voyage tu _____ assez _____ (ne
   manger pas) assez. Tu _____ (devenir) maigre.
   (skinny)

8. L'été dernier, toutes mes fleurs _____
   (mourir)

35C. Translate the following sentences using the correct verb in
the past tense.

   1. They went to the beach last weekend.

   2. I got into the taxi but I forgot my bag.

   3. Betty came to the house with her daughter.

   4. The boys left at midnight.

5. My grandfather died at the age of 95. (à l'age de...)

6. Céline arrived from the party after midnight.

7. We went to all of the boutiques in the town.

8. I took car out of the garage to clean it (the car).

Barb: Regarde, c'est notre voisin, Fred.

Joe: Bonjour, Fred. Comment ça va?

Fred: Très bien. Et vous ? Avez-vous pris des vacances ?

Barb: Oui, nous sommes revenus de France samedi
          dernier.

Fred: De France? C'est formidable! Vous y êtes restés
          combien de temps?

Joe: Nous sommes partis il y a trois semaines. Nous
          sommes restés en France pendant deux semaines.

Fred: Qu'est-ce que vous avez vu là-bas ?

Barb: Nous sommes arrivés à Paris le 15 août et on est resté
          une semaine. Puis, nous avons pris le train pour aller
          en Provence, où nous sommes restés encore une
          semaine dans une auberge.

Fred: Qu'est-ce que vous préférez, Paris ou la Provence ?

Joe: C'est très difficile à dire. Les deux sont très
          différentes. La grande ville et La Côte d'Azur.

Barb: Je n'ai pas voulu choisir. Alors, on a fait les deux!

Additional vocabulary

C'est formidable!   That's great!

il y a: in the present, this means there is/there are.
                      But in the past tense it means "ago"

là-bas: over there

puis: then...

encore: another, again, still

une auberge: an inn

la Cote d'Azur: the French Riviera

les deux: both

TO DO: Write a dialogue similar to the one above, using the past tense with both être and avoir as auxiliaries.

Appendix A   Answer Keys for Exercises

Chapter 4   Genders, Articles and Some Nouns

4A.

1. The girl
2. The meal
3. An office
4. The dog
5. A bike

4B

1. Le village
2. L'alliance (feminine)
3. La sonnette
4. Le garage
5. Le chateau
6. La jeunesse
7. L'idéalisme (masculine)
8. Le journal
9. La matinée
10. La mise à jour
11. La quantité
12. Le billet
13. Le salon
14. Le moment
15. La valise

16. La diversité

17. Le chapeau

18. Le tennis

Chapter 5   **Plurals of Nouns**

5A

1. les filles
2. un livre
3. une histoire
4. des gâteaux
5. les poissons
6. une bouteille
7. les chapeaux
8. des parcs
9. les hôpitaux
10. des bureaux
11. des choix
12. le voisin
13. des journaux
14. la fenêtre
15. les fils

Chapter 6   **The Verb "Etre"**

6A

Nous sommes...

Les chiens sont...

Elles sont...

Vous êtes...

Les voisins sont...

Les gens sont...

Le gâteau est...

La maison est...

Tu es...

6B

Le gâteau est délicieux.

Nous sommes fatigués.

Les voisins sont riches.

Le garçon est timide.

L'homme est intelligent.

Tu es intéressant.

La femme est malade.

Vous êtes têtus.

Chapter 9   **Aller: To Go**

9A.

1.   Il va à la piscine
2.   Nous allons au restaurant
3.   Je vais à l'école.
4.   Les enfants vont au parc.
5.   Vous allez au stade.
6.   On va au supermarché.
7.   Je vais à la boutique de chaussures.
8.   Ma mère va à la boulangerie acheter une baguette.
9.   La professeur va au bureau.
10. Nous allons tous au travail.

Chapter 10

Conjunctions, Words of frequency, and Small Words

10A

Au printemps, j'aime aller **à la** plage. Il y a **moins de** gens et il n'est pas **trop** chaud. **D'habitude**, je vais avec des amis. Aujourd'hui, **pourtant**, je vais là-bas seul. **Il y a** un beau soleil et **un peu** de vent. **Avant** d'arriver, j'achète un sandwich pour faire un pique-nique. **C'est très** agréable de prendre un pique-nique **sur** le sable.

Quand j'ai **assez de** soleil, je rentre chez moi, **mais** cette fois-ci je vais voir mon ami. Il va commander une pizza **avec** de la salade et nous allons regarder un film. Nous passons **toujours** un bon moment ensemble.

Chapter 11   **IR Regular Verbs**

11A

1. Ils choisissent une couleur pour la maison.
2. Nous finissons le projet avant le soir.
3. Vous remplissez le papier.   Tu remplis le papier.
4. Je réfléchis à son idée.
5. Les garçons réussissent à finir le programme

Chapter 12   **Avoir**

12A

1. Ils ont deux chats.
1. Nous avons très peu de temps.
2. J'ai du travail dans un restaurant.
3. Vous avez des enfants ?
4. Il a souvent des amis chez lui.
5. Tu as des beaux cheveux.

12B

1. J'ai une mauvaise note. I have a bad grade
2. La fête a lieu vendredi soir. The party takes place Friday evening.
3. Les garçons ont envie d'une pizza. The boys want pizza.
4. Nous avons besoin des clés. We need some keys.
5. Elle a souvent froid. She's often cold.
6. On a chaud! Ouvrez la fenêtre! We're hot ! Open the window!
7. Tu as l'air déprimé. Qu'est-ce qu'il y a? You look depressed. What's wrong ?
8. Vous avez toujours raison. You are always right.

Chapter 13 Negatives

13A

Practice with Negatives

1. Les filles ne dansent pas très souvent.
2. La lampe n'est pas jolie.
3. D'habitude ce magasin n'est pas ouvert.
4. Charles ne parle pas beaucoup.
5. Nous ne marchons pas dans le parc.

13B

Other types of negative phrases

1. Mes voisins ne travaillent jamais dans le jardin.
2. Je n'ai pas le temps de regarder l'émission.
3. Il n'y a plus de neige devant la maison.
4. Je ne vois personne a la caisse.
5. Nous n'étudions pas pendant le week-end.
6. Ellen n'a plus de jus d'orange.
7. Il n'y a personne dans cette chaise.
8. Mon fils ne finit jamais ses devoirs.

9. Elle n'a rien dans ses poches.
10. Il n'y a rien de bon à la télé ce soir.
11. Mon chef ne dit jamais la vérité.

Chapter 14   **Adjectives**

14A

1. Les garçons intelligents
2. Un livre interessant
3. Une feuille blanche
4. Des chaussures bleues
5. Un matin frais
6. Une femme tunisienne
7. Un chien paresseux
8. Un journal français
9. Une rue sèche
10. L'homme triste

14B

1. La voiture rouge
2. La jolie fille
3. La tarte délicieuse
4. Une vieille maison blanche/ Des vieilles maisons blanches
5. La dame italienne
6. Une voisine sympathique/ gentille
7. Une grande famille
8. Un haut bâtiment
9. Une robe verte
10. Le vieux chat gris
11. Des chiens méchants
12. Les papiers jaunes

Chapter 15 — These, Those, His, and Hers: Demonstrative & Possessive Adjectives

15A — Demonstrative

1. Cette voiture
2. Ce vélo
3. Ces amis
4. Ce matin
5. Cette idée
6. Ce garçon
7. Cet ordinateur
8. Ces portes
9. Ces insectes
10. Ces chausettes

Possessive Adjectives

15 B

1. Mon fils
2. Ton chat
3. Notre avis
4. Leurs enfants
5. Sa robe
6. Sa botte
7. Ses bottes
8. Mes tomates
9. Notre père
10. Leur camion

Chapter 16 — Food and Restaurants

16A

1. Je vais acheter du poulet.
2. Il mange du gâteau après chaque repas.
3. Jean-Luc aime la pizza.
4. Nous prenons du lait avec notre céréale.
5. Ils mangent des sandwiches pour le déjeuner.

6. Je prend de la crème dans mon café.
7. Mes cousins adorent manger de la glace en été.
8. Elle veut du Coca/ Elle veut un Coca (2 possibilities)
9. Nous prenons une carafe d'eau/Nous allons prendre une carafe d'eau.
10. Je voudrais du vin blanc.
11. Ma mère cherche des bananes et des pommes.
12. Sébastien va prendre de la bière/ une bière

Chapter 17   Asking Questions

17A

1. (intonation) Simone est malade?
   (est-ce que) Est-ce que Simone est malade?
   (inversion) Simone est-elle malade ?

2. Vous avez un billet?
   Est-ce que vous avez un billet?
   Avez-vous un billet?

3. Tu aimes la musique classique?
   Est-ce que tu aimes la musique classique ?
   Aimes-tu la musique classique?

4. Ils viennent au dîner?
   Est-ce qu'ils viennent au dîner ?
   Viennent-ils au dîner ?

5. Nous sommes en retard?
   Est-ce que nous sommes en retard?
   Sommes-nous en retard?

17B Fill in the blank with the word or words that fit.

- Combien de pommes avez-vous?
- Comment vas-tu arriver ? En train ou en voiture ?
- Combien d'argent est-ce qu'ils ont ?
- Comment (Quand, Pourquoi) vont-elles préparer le repas ?

- Pourquoi est-ce que vous avez peur ?
- Comment (Pourquoi, Où, Quand) est-ce que tu joues des cuillères ?
- Où vas-tu ? Comment vas-tu ?
- Où sont mes livres ?
- Pourquoi est-ce que vous parlez très fort ?
- Quand est-ce que vous allez arriver ?

Chapter 19   RE Regular Verbs

19B

1. Nous attendons le rendez-vous.
2. Tu perds toujours ta clé.
3. J'entends la musique du voisin.
4. Il rend le livre à la bibliothèque.
5. Les garçons défendent leur petit frère à l'école.
6. Ils vendent la maison à la plage.

Chapter 22   Weather and Leisure

22A

1. Nous faisons
2. Ils font
3. Je fais, je ne fais pas
4. Tu ne fais pas
5. Vous faites
6. Faire

Chapter 23   Telling Time

23A. (you can add du matin, du soir for clarity if needed)

Il est neuf heures vingt

Il est deux heures et demie.

Il est cinq heures moins le quart. Il est quatre heures quarante-cinq.

Il est sept heure trente-cinq.

Il est neuf heures cinquante. Il est dix heures moins dix.

Il est midi.

Il est midi vingt.

23B   24-hour clock

Il est seize heures quarante.   16h40

Il est huit heures. 8h00

Il est dix-huit heures quinze. 18h15

Il est onze heures trente. 11h30

Il est vingt-quatre heures 24h00

Il est vingt-deux heures. 22h00

Chapter 24   Numbers 61-100/ Expressing Dates

24A

79: soixante-dix-neuf   65: soixante-cinq

124 : cent vingt-quatre   85 : quatre-vingt-cinq

90 : quatre-vingt-dix   77 : soixante-dix-sept

82 : quatre-vingt-deux   150 : cent cinquante

250 : deux cent cinquante   320 : trois cent vingt

188

24B Dates

1824 : dix-huit cent vingt-quatre/ mil huit cent vingt-quatre

1750 : dix-sept cent cinquante/ mil sept cent cinquante

1200 : douze cents/ mil deux cents

1998 : dix-neuf cent quatre-vingt dix-huit/ mil neuf cent quatre-vingt dix-huit

2005 : deux mille cinq

1961 : dix-neuf cent soixante et un/ mil neuf cent soixante et un

1599 : quinze cent quatre-vingt-dix-neuf/ mil cinq cent quatre-vingt-dix-neuf

1450 : quatorze cent cinquante/ mil quatre cent cinquante

Chapter 25   Comparatives of adjectives and quantities

25A   Adjectives

1. Le chat est plus gros que le chien.
2. Sallie est moins heureuse que Claire.
3. Nous sommes aussi occupés que nos enfants.
4. Les robes sont moins chères que les jupes.
5. Ce vin est plus sec que le champagne.
6. Cet examen est moins difficile que l'autre.
7. Ma mère est moins calme que mon père.
8. Tu es aussi drôle que ton ami.

25.B

1. Adam est plus grand que Joe.
2. Je suis moins riche que mon frère.
3. Nous sommes plus occupés que nos amis.
4. Tu es aussi intelligent que moi.

189

5. Mon chien est plus petit que ton chat.
6. Sa voiture est aussi chère que ma maison.
7. Ils sont aussi intéressants que vous.
8. Vous êtes moins méchants que vous semblez.
9. Ces films sont plus intéressants que les livres.
10. Cette rue est moins large que l'avenue.

25.C   Superlatives

1. Ce vélo est le plus cher dans le magasin.
2. Il a la meilleure collection des livres.
3. Ellen est la plus occupée de tous mes amis. (or toutes mes amies, in feminine)
4. C'est le plus mauvais jour de ma vie !
5. Ce film est le meilleur du festival.
6. Madame Trudeau est la prof la plus gentille de l'école.

25D   Comparing quantities

1. Ils ont plus d'argent que moi.
2. Les voisins regardent moins de films que nous.
3. Nous buvons autant de vin que nos enfants.
4. J'ai autant que vous.
5. Elle a plus de vêtements que sa sœur.

25. E   Comparing quantities

1. Elle boit moins d'eau que moi.
2. Hope a moins de patience que sa sœur.
3. Evelyne mange moins de pâtisserie que son mari.
4. Nous avons moins de temps qu'avant. (avant = before)
5. Les enfants ont moins de jouets que l'année dernière.

Chapter 27   **Comparing Adverbs**

27 A.

1. Jeanne travaille moins que Fred.
2. Mes amis dansent plus souvent que moi.
3. Christophe court plus lentement que Rémy.
4. Stéphane cuisine aussi mal que son frère.

190

5. Ils voyagent moins que moi. (or moins souvent que moi)
6. J'étudie autant que Jean-Marc.
7. Elle parle plus lentement que sa mère.
8. Nous aimons marcher autant que vous.

Chapter 31   **Direct Object Pronouns**

31A

1. Je descends la valise. Je la descends.
2. Nous cherchons l'adresse. Est-ce que tu la sais?
3. Il y a des chiens mignons dans le parc. Vous les voyez ?
4. Ces gâteaux ont l'air bon, mais je ne les achètes pas.
5. Mon professeur n'est pas gentil. Je ne l'aime pas.
6. Voici la clé. Prenez-la !
7. Vos bottes sont sales. Ne les mettez pas à l'intérieur.
8. Le vélo est dans le garage, mais je ne le trouve pas.

31B

1. Est-ce que tu m'écoutes ? Tu m'écoutes ?
2. Mes voisins sont sympas. Je les vois dans leur jardin chaque après-midi.
3. Tes parents te cherchent.
4. La danseuse est très bonne. J'aime la regarder.
5. Je vous invite chez moi ce week-end.
6. Elle appelle ses amis maintenant. Elle les appelle souvent.
7. Mon grand-père nous amène dans la campagne chaque été.
8. Ma sœur m'attends devant l'église.

Chapter 32   **Indirect Object Pronouns**

32A

1. Elle lui donne la lettre.
2. Olivier lui achète une nouvelle voiture.
3. Le directeur nous donne la réponse.
4. Ils vous expliquent le processus.

5. Le comité va me répondre demain.
6. Il lui écrit souvent.
7. Nous leur répondons la semaine prochaine.
8. Je te donne les clés maintenant.

Chapter 33   Expressing desires, abilities, or obligations

33A

1. De notre chambre d'hôtel, nous pouvons voir les montagnes.
2. Les garçons doivent finir leurs devoirs avant de sortir.
3. Si tu veux, je peux faire le repas.
4. Mon frère préfère/veut voir le nouveau film de Spielberg.
5. Je ne peux pas déjeuner avec toi demain. Je dois aller chez le coiffeur.
6. Les filles peuvent/ veulent voir le film avec nous.
7. Est-ce que vous voulez prendre un dessert ?
8. Vous ne pouvez pas vous garer ici. C'est interdit.
9. Attendez, je vous dois de l'argent.
10. Qu'est-ce que vous voulez faire ce soir ?

Chapter 34   Past Tense with Avoir

34A   Regular verbs

1. Mes sœurs ont déjeuné chez notre tante.
2. Joey a attendu ses amis devant le cinéma.
3. Nous avons joué aux cartes jusqu'à minuit.
4. Tu as aimé ton cadeau.
5. Elle a rempli la bouteille.
6. Vous avez parlé du problème.
7. J'ai cherché tes chaussures mais je n'ai rien trouvé.
8. Tu as fini ton projet ?
9. Hier matin il a travaillé dans le jardin.
10. Ils ont rendu leurs devoirs en avance.

34B   Irregular verbs

1. Nous avons eu des problemes avec la voiture.
2. J'ai été à Chicago le week-end dernier.
3. Avez-vous bu tout le vin rouge ?
4. Lionel a vu des enfants dans la rue.
5. J'ai pu finir mon programme en six mois.
6. Thierry a voulu venir avec nous au cinéma, mais il a dû travailler.

34C   Regular and irregular verbs

1. Nous avons acheté des chaussures le week-end dernier.
2. Le restaurant a servi le déjeuner jusqu'à quatorze heures.
3. Hier mon ami a perdu ses clés.
4. Ses enfants ont pu visiter l'hôpital.
5. Samedi soir Alice a dormi dans le jardin.
6. J'ai vu le film trois fois.
7. Nous avons bu beaucoup d'eau après le match de tennis.
8. Il a connu ce garçon au lycée.

Chapter 35   Past Tense with Etre

35A.

1. Joël est allé au stade avec son frère.
2. Nous sommes entrés dans le restaurant.
3. Ma grand-mère est née en 1920.
4. L'homme est descendu du taxi.
5. Les filles sont sorties avec leurs amies à la fête.
6. Quand êtes-vous arrivé? (formal) Quand êtes-vous arrivés ?(Plural)
7. Marion est passée chez moi trés tôt ce matin.
8. Leurs cousins sont revenus des vacances dimanche soir.

35B.
1. Nous sommes passés au magasin et nous avons acheté du lait.
2. Le weekend dernier, mes voisins du quartier ont mangé ensemble.
3. Ce matin, j'ai sorti la poubelle.
4. L'été dernier ma famille est allée en Grèce.
5. Esther est tombée dans l'escalier.
6. Ces gens ont voulu aller avant nous.
7. Pendant le voyage tu n'as pas assez mangé. Tu es devenu maigre.
8. L'été dernier toutes mes fleurs sont mortes.

35C.

1. Ils sont allés à la plage le weekend dernier.
2. Je suis monté (e) dans le taxi mais j'ai oublié mon sac.
3. Betty est venue à la maison avec sa fille.
4. Les garçons sont partis à minuit.
5. Mon grand-père est mort à l'âge de 95.
6. Céline est arrivée de la fête après minuit.
7. Nous sommes allés à toutes les boutiques dans la ville.
8. J'ai sorti la voiture du garage pour la nettoyer.

Appendix B   Resources for Travelers

Travel Resources*

www.OliversFrance.com My website to help you find new places in France to visit that you might not have thought of! Travel tips and more.

Trains

SNCF Train schedules, including TGV: https://en.oui.sncf/en/ Also, https://www.raileurope.com/destinations/country-guides/article/france-10

Eurail Europe passes: www.eurail.com/

France Rail: https://www.raileurope.ca/rail-tickets-passes/france-pass/index.html (ticketing fee added)

Here's a helpful article by Rick Steves on train options in France:

https://www.ricksteves.com/travel-tips/transportation/trains/france-rail-passes

TER Regional Trains (by SNCF): www.sncf.com/en/passenger-offer/travel-by-train/ter

Driving

Tolls in France: www.autoroutes.fr/en/key-rates.htm

Driving distances: https://bit.ly/2yQMirn

Inter-Europe Airlines

Ryan Air: www.ryanair.com Limited routes in France but includes Paris, Nice, Biarritz, and Tours. Flights to UK and Ireland.

Easy Jet: www.easyjet.com Destinations to many large cities in France: Strasbourg, Bordeaux, Lyon, Toulouse, Marseille and others. Goes to Corsica as well.

195

Wizz Air: www.wizzair.com (leaves from Paris and goes eastbound; not useful for travel within France.)

Corsair: www.corsair.fr/en Flies to 18 cities in France and elsewhere in the French-speaking world.

Air France: www.airfrance.us

Airport Transportation (Paris airports)

Transportation into Paris from Charles de Gaulle airport

Roissy Bus: https://easycdg.com/roissybus-paris-cdg-de-gaulle-airport/

Air France shuttle: http://transfer.airport-paris.com/air-france-coach-service.htm You don't have to be traveling with Air France in order to use this shuttle service.

RER B: This is a train that goes from the CDG airport into the center of Paris about every 10-15 minutes. You can get off at at Gare du Nord or Châtelet for any other stop along the RER B and change to a Métro line. Cost: 10.30 euros. (7 euros for children.)

Maps of Paris:

Downloadable Metro Map: https://www.ratp.fr/en/plans-lignes/plan-metro
Downloadable city map: http://en.parisinfo.com/how-to-get-to-and-around-paris/maps-and-plans this downloads a map of Paris (streets) which you can zoom in or out or move around to show where you want. It's provided by the city of Paris. Click on "Paris Map" and scroll down under the section "Street Plans", or maps.

For extensive information on things to do in Paris, please refer to my book *Magical Paris: Over 100 Things to Do Across Paris*.

Hotels

In Paris: http://en.parisinfo.com

Around France: www.france-hotel-guide.com/en/

Gîte: a gîte is a private home (usually in rural areas) that is rented out to tourists. www.gites-de-france.com/en / or www.gite.com

This is a respectable chain of lodging all over France www.logishotels.com/en/

Specialty trips

Small Group tours

Provence: Simply France with Dawn
http://www.simplyfrancewithdawn.com

Groups of four to eight people visit Provence for thematic tours, including small town Provence, wine tours, and cooking tours.

Blueroads Touring
www.blueroadstouring.com/tours/europe/france Maximum group size of 18

Cooking tours around France (International Kitchen)
www.theinternationalkitchen.com/cooking-vacations/france/ See more ideas in *Oliver's France* website.

French Escapades https://frenchescapade.com Cooking, painting, or cultural tours

River and Barge Cruises

Canal du Midi, other French waterways www.leBoat.com

www.avalonwaterways.com (Many European destinations)

http://www.french-waterways.com

Bike and walking tours

www.utracks.com You can choose a walking, hiking or biking tour, or combine one of these with a barge cruise. Hiking tours through the French countryside, vineyards, forests, beaches and mountains. Some tours are family-friendly.

Books

Magical Paris: Over 100 Things to Do Across Paris by K. B. Oliver. Unlike other guides, this one covers the **entire** city of Paris. It's perfect for getting off the beaten track.

A French Garden: The Loire Valley by K. B. Oliver. This is a concise and yet complete guide to this enchanted place just an hour from Paris.

I like Fodors and Rick Steves for an overview of cities and suggestions for excursions and hotels. They both cover the main sites as well as a few others.

Language Learning Resources

Barron's Mastering French Vocabulary: A Thematic Approach

501 French Verbs (with CD) by Christopher Kendris. There are other verb conjugation books that are also good.

Coffee Break French https://radiolingua.com/coffeebreakfrench

Duo-Lingo https://www.duolingo.com/course/fr/en/Learn-French-Online

French with Vincent: You Tube videos for pronunciation

Word of the Day http://www.transparent.com/word-of-the-day/today/french.html

* Listed resources are not necessarily vetted by the author

Appendix C *The Project*

You want to go to France. The best way to prepare ahead (and the best way to increase your chances of going) is to create an itinerary and a rough budget. At this point it's all tentative, so go ahead and dream! But do all the research as if it's already on the schedule...and maybe it will be!

Here are some steps that you'll find helpful

1. Decide what time of year you'd like to go and how long you'll spend

2. Decide what cities/regions you want to visit and how long you'll spend in each place. Consult maps and websites to get ideas.

3. Choose your modes of transportation (rental car? TGV train? TER regional trains? Plane?) You may want several.

4. Look up typical routes and fares and note these. Note also the average travel time between destinations.

5. What kinds of lodging do you want? A bed and breakfast? An inn? A room in someone's home? A big hotel chain or a small one? Maybe you're looking for a tour, or a package of some kind. Maybe you'd like to rent an apartment as a home base and travel from there on day trips.

6. Next look up some hotels online that correspond to the type you are looking for. Note the average prices for the season you are traveling. How many nights will you spend in each place? Note this on your budget.

7. Are there special things you'd like to do, such as take a bike tour, a barge cruise, visit a chateau, take a cooking class, visit some vineyards, do some educational visits (the chocolate museum, the perfume museum, etc.)

8. Think about your restaurant budget. What is your preference? Some people like to sample the best restaurants available. Others will do a few, but simple restaurants or picnics the rest of the time. Don't forget about bakeries and farmers' markets, which are wonderful in France. That can reduce your food budget if you think of that for some of your meals.

9. Lastly, make a list of your top "must see/must do" items, if you have these. For example, *must do* a wine-tasting; *must see* the Louvre.)

10. Gather brochures, photos, text from websites, links to relevant sites and videos. Preview your destinations on You Tube, or Google Images if you like.

These ideas will help you create a great itinerary for your next visit to France. If you can't go within the foreseeable future, keep all of your information in a file somewhere as your "dream folder," with the intention to make it reality as soon as you can!

Bon Voyage!

Thank you for purchasing *Real French for Travelers*. If you have suggestions for future editions, or if you find an error or have a question, feel free to contact me at:

Info@Oliversfrance.com

If you enjoyed Real French for Travelers and found it helpful, please consider leaving a review to help others discover it. Thank you!

K. B. Oliver

Photo on page 5 is Nice. Photo on page 19 is the Latin Quarter area of Paris.

For new ideas of places to see in France, visit
www.Oliversfrance.com

Sign up for twice-monthly email posts (and a free e-book on food specialties across France!)

For your next trip to Paris, you can't do without *Magical Paris: Over 100 Things to do Across Paris*, also by K. B. Oliver.

Most guide books cover the same famous monuments. This book gives you those as well as so many things to do across *all* 20 districts of this unforgettable city. Why not enjoy ALL of Magical Paris!

See the next page...

201

All across Paris...discover the magic.

This booklet has both, updated information on the places you most want to see, as well as some places you've never read about anywhere. Helpful descriptions, maps and photos as well as the insider favorites from a longtime Paris resident are within these pages.

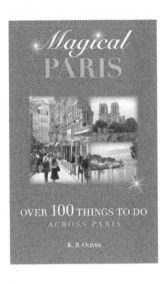

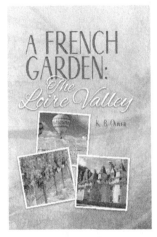

An Unforgettable French Garden

Just over an hour from Paris you'll find an enchanted valley filled with medieval and Renaissance castles, vineyards, great food, and charming towns. This guide is concise yet complete, covering the whole Loire Valley. Just the guide you need for your trip.

About the Author

K. B. Oliver lived in France for 13 years, primarily in Paris and its suburbs. Currently she writes fiction and nonfiction and teaches French in North Carolina. She also posts regularly on her blog, Oliver's France.

202